Praise for *The Sinner's Guide to Natural Family Planning*

I admire Simcha Fisher's work, and have found her thoughts on NFP very sensible. Her take on family life and Catholicism is humorous, loving and honest.
— Dr. Janet Smith, author of *Contraception: Why Not?*

Faithful, funny, and honest. Simcha addresses the obstacles couples face in living out the blessings and challenges of natural family planning. Readers will appreciate her frank and heartfelt take on this sensitive subject.
— Dr. Gregory Popcak, author of *Holy Sex!*

Simcha speaks ... with honesty along with the wit and wisdom that always make her teachings so memorable and helpful. She summons all of us to trust, mutual patience, and kindness, and to a joyful honesty about NFP.
— Msgr. Charles Pope, Pastor of Holy Comforter – St. Cyprian Parish, Washington, D.C.

G. K. Chesterton once said, "A thing worth doing is worth doing badly." And anyone practicing NFP knows what he means (hence the appropriate verb: practice.) In this excellent and witty book, Simcha Fisher unveils the joys, benefits, and the inconvenient difficulties of natural family planning. Refreshingly honest and joyful, the result is a desperately needed resource. All couples should read this book.
— Brandon Vogt, author of *The Church and New Media*

This is not a book about how to chart your cycle or how your body works, it's a book about how human nature and husbands and wives work. Clear writing, refreshing logic, profound wisdom, practical, detailed advice, and *laugh-out-loud humor* (hooray!) make this unlike any other NFP book you have ever read.
— Leila Miller of *Little Catholic Bubble*

Fisher is wide-awake; she appreciates irony and—with a sense of humor that is proportionate to the seriousness of her purpose—she helps the reader wake up and smell the irony, too…NFP is not free. It costs a great deal, of both partners. And yet…through the very depths of her learned compassion—expressed so eloquently and with such transparent humility—Fisher provides the evidence of its solid, life-enhancing value.

— Elizabeth Scalia, author of
Strange Gods: Unmasking the Idols in Everyday Life

With advice on how to realistically and lovingly practice marital chastity to how to talk to your husband, and packed with solid Church teaching accompanied by Ms. Fisher's characteristic humor and wit, *The Sinner's Guide to Natural Family Planning* should become a recommended resource in every NFP teacher's arsenal.

— Kayla Peterson, co-founder of iuseNFP.com

Before *The Sinner's Guide to Natural Family Planning*, the only way you could get this kind of candor on the subject of natural family planning was in private conversations with your best friend. Simcha has taken all the things we think about NFP but feel like we can't say, brought them into the light, and addressed them with insight and razor-sharp wit. You'll laugh, you'll nod your head in recognition, and you'll ultimately walk away inspired by the kind of encouragement that only someone else in the trenches can offer.

— Jennifer Fulwiler of Conversion Diary

I expected the funny parts. I didn't expect to need a box of tissues sitting next to me as I read. Simcha mixes the perfect cocktail of great humor, profound insights, down-to-earth wisdom, and practical advice. This book is sorely needed, and I'm glad Simcha is the one who wrote it.

— Melanie Bettinelli of The Wine-Dark Sea

If you've ever lost your head about Catholic teaching on sex, Simcha Fisher is here to screw it back on. Even if you've been reading Simcha for years, you haven't heard her this candid and this in-depth about all the things you've ever privately wondered about natural family planning and how people make it work. I wish I'd had this book a decade ago.

— Elizabeth Duffy, Patheos blogger
(www.patheos.com/blogs/duffy/)

Too often NFP is sold to young couples, just like the health-and-wealth gospel is sold to Christians who are in debt—*God will bless you with unicorns and rainbows*! Too bad this isn't true for most NFP-using couples. Simcha Fisher's new book isn't going to make NFP any easier, but it is full of hope, laughter, and the truth about the good news of Jesus Christ. My only regret is that I didn't have this book when I was a newlywed. It might have prevented me from wanting to burn certain charts.

— Marcel LeJeune, author of *Set Free to Love:
Lives Changed by the Theology of the Body*

I am the first person to admit that my husband and I have drunk the NFP Kool-Aid. But I wholeheartedly endorse the attitude in this book. It's frank, it's conversational, it's funny, and—possibly most important—it firmly rejects the nosy judgmentalism that currently pervades the conversation, choosing instead to emphasize the great variety of good paths that a couple may find as they discern together the right decisions for their family.

— Erin Arlinghaus of Bearing Blog

With honesty and clarity Simcha Fisher illuminates a truth many people would rather forget: that in this fallen world made up of sinful and broken people, all relationships, including marriage, can either be strengthened in the shadow of the Cross or destroyed on the altars of the false gods of selfishness.

— Erin Manning of And Sometimes Tea
and author of *Tales of Telmaja*

The SINNER'S GUIDE *to* NATURAL FAMILY PLANNING

By Simcha Fisher

Our Sunday Visitor Publishing Division
Our Sunday Visitor, Inc.
Huntington, Indiana 46750

To Damien, duh

CONTENTS

INTRODUCTION

Why This Book, and What It's Not

As I write the final chapters of this book, it's Natural Family Planning Awareness Week. Each July, the Internet becomes gooey with information about NFP. Frankly, what I want more than anything is to be a little less aware of NFP.

So why did I write this book?

Well, couples who use natural family planning to space pregnancies are happier, more satisfied, and more faithful than their contraception-using peers. Each month, they enjoy a deliriously romantic "honeymoon effect." Men spend fertile phases chastely courting their wives, who eagerly await infertile days so that they can joyously give of themselves to their husbands.

Just like at your house, right? Or maybe not.

Maybe it's more like this: You love each other, but your sex life is kind of a mess. You refuse contraception out of obedience to Church teaching, and you truly believe that natural family planning is better than those awful chemicals everyone else uses anyway. You're doing everything right…but having no fun at all. Your husband is angry and frustrated, you're bitter and perplexed, and the whole thing has somehow become an aching knot of mis-understandings, hurt feelings, and alienation. When you read the glowing reports of the marriage-building benefits of natural family planning, they only make you laugh. Or cry.

How natural is that?

It may not be natural, but it's very common. And that's why I wrote this book.

The truth is that the marriage-building benefits of remaining faithful to Church teaching are real. They are attainable. It's just that you have to work hard to get them.

NFP boosters tend to paint a rosy picture because it's a hard sell, persuading people to turn their sex lives over to God. And so, not wanting to scare anyone off, they emphasize the benefits while glossing over the sacrifices that often come along as a matched set.

I understand why they do this. You're not going to convert the masses by saying, "Hey, everybody! Who's ready for some redemptive suffering?" But so many couples launch into NFP expecting sunshine and buttercups, and are horrified to discover, instead, the Cross. Unprepared to make any changes, they end up resenting their spouses and the Church in general—or else they feel guilty and ashamed to be struggling, like there's something wrong with them for not lovin' every minute of it.

That's who this book is for. It's for couples who are completely dedicated to the idea; couples who, as long as they have a good reason to postpone pregnancy, will be using NFP to do so. But so far, they have found the fabulous side effects to be elusive; and by "elusive," I mean "horrible, horrible lies."

I don't love NFP. I don't think that it's a magical cure-all that every couple must embrace in order to achieve full humanity. And I wish that I didn't have to use it at all.

But I don't hate it like I used to. Now I understand what people are talking about when they say it's "marriage-building."

My husband and I have been married for fifteen years, we have nine children, and we've used NFP off and on. In those years, we've tried, with varying degrees of effort and success, to space pregnancies; and we've struggled, with varying degrees of effort and success, against the spiritual growth that the Holy Spirit keeps trying to sneak onto our plates when we're not looking.

We always wanted a big family, and we hope to have at least a few more kids before we go kaput, fertility-wise. On the outside, we have always looked like a happy, holy, cooperative, trusting, generous model of Catholic marriage and family life—but on the inside, we used to be a mess. We were immature and selfish and lacking in self-control. We had no clue about each other's needs, or how to open our lives to God, or how to balance prudence and trust, or how to see children as gifts. We loved each other and our kids, but we were making each other miserable.

And now we're…better.

Could these benefits have come to us without NFP? Who knows? It's not as if God has one method for making us holier, and if we don't get on board with that one method, then we're out of luck.

I do know that we've come far, as a couple and as Catholics. And our experience of NFP makes a handy jumping-off place to explain all the changes we have gone through. I want to share what we've learned, and to put a little balance and honesty into the conversation about NFP.

And I want to give you hope. If you're struggling with NFP, it's not because you're a crappy person, or because the Church doesn't understand what sex is like in real life. It's because, for some people, NFP is a genuine and significant cross. As with any cross, you can collapse under its weight, or you can carry it and let it make you stronger. But unlike many crosses, you can choose to put it down.

But if it's your lot, right now, to carry this cross, then read on! Let me tell you what this book is not about:

- It's not going to tell you how to chart.
- It's not going to spell out the theological argument against contraception.
- It's not going to make a secular case for NFP. I'm Catholic, and I write like a Catholic, so there.
- It won't pretend that NFP will fix your marriage if your marriage is in serious trouble.

- It's not going to tell you how many children to have.
- It will not tell you that all married couples should automatically use NFP, and it will not suggest that couples who use NFP are either superior or inferior to couples who just take whatever comes.
- It's not going to deal with infertility or other health problems, even though many people turn to NFP seeking healing for these things.
- It will not talk a lot about children. Instead, this book focuses on sexual and relationship issues. For balance, just imagine that, as I write about sex, desire, obedience, and passion, I'm nursing the baby, and there's a five-year-old sitting on my head, and a toddler carefully fitting peanuts between my toes.

Finally, if you read my words and get so intellectually inflamed that you rush right home to your spouse and have a deep and penetrating discussion about what you've learned here, please remember that "Simcha" is a beautiful, timeless name that is suitable for both baby boys and baby girls.

PART I

NFP AND YOUR SPIRITUAL LIFE

CHAPTER I

———

Why Doesn't the Church Just Make a List?

When Catholics talk about NFP—specifically, about legitimate reasons to use NFP to avoid pregnancy—someone
always asks rather plaintively why the Church doesn't just clear
up all the confusion. Why not just make a list: on the right, good
reasons for postponing a pregnancy; on the left, bad reasons?

Obviously we should still pray and try to discern God's will
for us—but why does it have to be so vague? Why doesn't the
Church just give us a break and spell it out already?

Most of those who want more clarity are genuine seekers of
God's will, looking for guidance as they discern the best path for
their marriage. Others are looking for a definitive document to
prove that their neighbors are abusing NFP by using it with a
"contraceptive mentality."

The Church does, of course, give us guidelines. In *Humanae
Vitae* it says:

> If therefore there are well-grounded reasons for spacing
> births, arising from the physical or psychological condi-
> tion of husband or wife, or from external circumstances,
> the Church teaches that married people may then take
> advantage of the natural cycles immanent in the repro-
> ductive system and engage in marital intercourse only
> during those times that are infertile, thus controlling
> birth… (16)

And the Catechism says: "For just reasons, spouses may wish to space the births of their children. It is their duty to make certain that their desire is not motivated by selfishness, but is in conformity with the generosity appropriate to responsible parenthood..." (*Catechism of the Catholic Church*, 2368).

In his Address to the Italian Catholic Union of Midwives, Pope Pius XII says that serious motives, such as "medical, eugenic, economic, and social" reasons "which not rarely arise" can exempt a couple from the obligation of bearing children.

But we're still left with those adjectives: well-grounded, serious, just. What does that mean? Why doesn't the Church give some specific examples of what qualifies as a just reason?

Well, one problem is that my just reason is not necessarily the same as your just reason.

For instance, we could say, "Severe economic instability is a good reason to postpone pregnancy." But...

Woman (A) grew up deathly poor, and fully expected to die before she hit age 40. Her husband is disabled and often out of work, and sometimes they have to scramble for the rent on their tiny house. But this is routine and tolerable for them, and causes no turmoil. With help from friends and government programs, they are raising reasonably happy, healthy children on $25,000 a year.

Woman (B) grew up wealthy, has always generously endowed Crisis Pregnancy Centers in her town, and always hoped to have a large family of her own. But a catastrophe struck, she went bankrupt, and now she has to sell everything and move into a tiny house and live on $25,000 a year. They're still reeling from the shock of what their life has become, and are trying to learn how to accept help, rather than give it.

Woman (C) lives in a tiny house on $25,000 a year, which her husband manages thriftily, so no one is deprived. But she makes him sleep in one of those plastic dog igloos at the foot of her bed until he agrees to sell his beloved used book shop and take a real job at SoulDeth Inc., where he can make some real money.

Woman (D) recently quit her high-paying job so she can stay home and have babies. They now live on her husband's salary of $25,000 a year and can hardly wait to fill their tiny new house with children.

You see? Objectively, the circumstances are the same, and "severe economic instability" describes all four. But their attitude toward having another baby right then would be entirely different. It's not enough to say, "Lilies of the field and so on. We must trust God." That's not asking much from Woman (A), but it's asking heroism from Woman (B).

Or you could say, "Just trust God with your fertility! We're not in control of our lives; God is." But consider another set of women:

Woman (A) is fearful, anxious, rigid, and domineering. Her husband is a little bit afraid of her, and her confessor always urges her to trust God more.

Woman (B) is childish and weak, and tends to leave all the heavy thinking to her husband—and then feels sorry for herself when they suffer the consequences of his choices. Their marriage is miserable, and her confessor always tells her to be more of an adult.

Woman (C) is careless and selfish, and lacks self-control, and her confessor always tells her to use more prudence, take more responsibility.

Woman (D) tries with all her might to be as holy as the other women around her, and she keeps having more babies to prove her trust in God, even though her household is out of control and her children are neglected. Her confessor always tells her that God asks different things of different people, and to keep her eyes on her own work.

"Trusting God" is wonderful, but means something entirely different in each of these cases.

All right, so the Church allows more latitude than you may think when it comes to discerning family size. But surely, some matters are so trivial that they can't possibly constitute a legitimate reason to postpone a pregnancy. Weight, for instance, is rarely a life-and-death issue. It seems like we'd be safe in saying, "No, you shouldn't postpone a pregnancy just so you can lose a little weight." But even here, there can be much more than meets the eye—and the Church recognizes this.

Woman (A) is healthy and beautiful, but is married to a man who berates her nightly for not fitting into the jeans she wore in high school, even though that was twenty years and five babies ago. He has taught her to hate herself, and will torture her emotionally if she makes a charting mistake and gets pregnant.

Woman (B) preaches radical openness to life, but in her most honest moments will admit to herself that having lots of babies happens to be a fabulous excuse for never having to deal with her unhealthy attitudes toward food. After all, she can't possibly be bothered to think about her diet, because she's pregnant (or postpartum, or nursing…).

Woman (C) used to be anorexic, and with years of therapy and hard work has achieved a healthy weight. But being even five pounds over that healthy weight puts her in danger of a relapse, and the idea of another pregnancy gives her panic attacks.

Woman (D) is just a petty twit who wants to make her tubbier friends feel like killing themselves when they go swimsuit shopping together. No baby this year, not after all the money she put into that state-of-the-art bone-shaving surgery!

All four women are faced with Losing Weight vs. Having Another Baby; but the details couldn't be more different.

Or you could say, "A large family is a sign of God's blessing. You'll never regret having another baby!" Indisputable, right?

Woman (A) always wanted a big family, and happily gives birth three times in the first five years of her marriage. She looks forward to many more years of fertility.

Woman (B) always wanted a big family, but now that she has six children, and a few of them turned out to have special needs, she figures it would be a good idea to take a break. She also wants to work out a few problems in her marriage that have been brewing unresolved under the chaos for a few years.

Woman (C) always wanted a big family, and now has eleven children. She probably has another decade of fertility to go, but while she loves her kids dearly, she is just plain tired. She and her husband are much more financially and emotionally stable than they were when they started their family—and yet the idea of another pregnancy fills her with dread.

Woman (D) always wanted a big family and is on the verge of menopause—and suddenly feels a deep yearning for just one more baby, for reasons that would have been foreign to her twenty-five years ago, on her honeymoon.

The four women in this final example are, of course, all the same woman, at different stages in her life. She has always trusted God, and God has blessed her in different ways at different times. You see? You can't even apply a specific, inflexible, objective rule to one woman: there are still just too many variables. For any specific, objective rule you laid down, you could find exceptions which are within the realm of normal human circumstances.

Can we ever say that we have an indisputably good reason, or an indisputably bad reason, for postponing a pregnancy?

Of course. It's just that I can't think of anything more personal and private than these reasons. I believe that if the Church ever did give a specific, objective list of legitimate reasons for avoiding or achieving pregnancy, it would cause more confusion, not less.

People with good reasons to postpone a pregnancy would doubt themselves, and people with no good reason would find loopholes. People would judge each other even more than they already do (which is a shameful amount), and it would distract from the soul's conversation with God.

Yes, worldly, modernized couples need to hear someone say, "Marriage is for making children, and children are a privilege, not a burden. Don't squander the gift of your fertility, but seek the gifts that God is offering." But I grow more and more skeptical of the charge that, among the tiny fraction of Catholics who use NFP, most use it with a "contraceptive mentality."

The phrase originated with Pope John Paul II, who used it in *Familiaris Consortio* and then in *Evangelium Vitae* to describe a corrosive modern mindset, which not only encompasses a widespread acceptance of the use of literal contraception, but also lays the groundwork for other disastrous offences against the human person, such as abortion and sterilization. Where is the evidence that he was speaking of people who use NFP with the wrong motives? Nowhere. Nowhere at all.

It is possible to use NFP *selfishly*. But that's the sin of selfishness, not the sin of contraception, and no one has the right to invent new sins that never appear in any catechism or Church document.

But! you will say. It's so obvious sometimes! That couple I see ahead of me every Sunday at Mass? Maybe they're technically doing it right. Maybe they took their Pre-Cana classes from the diocese and got their certificate. But they only have one kid, and they're obviously pretty happy with things remaining that way. Come on! They have a shiny new car. They have fancy vacations, they have this and that. You don't have to be a mind reader to know just exactly what's going on inside *that* marriage. There's someone who's abusing NFP. There's someone who's following the letter of the law, but with a contraceptive mentality.

Okay, if you're so sure, then how about this: you don't have to be a mind reader to know what's going on inside marriages with seven or more children and a tired-looking wife. Clearly, those husbands are raping their wives every night.

What's that you say? That's a horrible accusation, completely untrue, and no one has a right to say that about your marriage? Well, maybe that's how it looks from the outside.

You see, it cuts both ways: if you can read the hearts of couples with only a few children, then I can read the hearts of couples with many. See how ugly that gets? Only one Person knows what's in another man's heart, and that person ain't you or me.

And for people who aren't out to judge anyone else, but just want clarity and guidance in their own lives, here's a cheering idea from my sister, Abigail Tardiff:

> The Church's moral teachings are a great gift, because they save us from the bad effects of innocent wrongdoings; they can stop us from unknowingly messing up our lives, if we're humble enough to listen. But they don't replace a tryst with the Creator—and who would want them to?

So if the Church seems distressingly vague, it's because she doesn't want to get in the way of the conversation you could be having with God. He doesn't just want to talk to The Church as a whole: He wants to talk to you.

And that's why the Church doesn't just make a list.

CHAPTER 2

Making Room

I wrote this essay right before Advent, about a month before my ninth baby was born. I included it here because sometimes people think that mothers of big families must be especially organized, especially prudent, especially joyful, especially generous, especially wealthy, or especially... something.

The truth is, most moms of big families are winging it just as often as anyone else. By God's grace and with breathing exercises, everything more or less turns out okay. It's all right to have mixed feelings about having another baby! The childbearing years are like one long Advent season: growing time.

*****

My youngest kids are finally getting the idea that there is a baby—not an image, or a concept, or one of those weird grown-up stories, but an actual human being—inside my belly. They can tell it's true, because they can see what is unmistakably a little baby butt, bopping around about eighteen degrees northwest of what used to be my belly button.

"But—" asked my kids, "But how is there room in there for a whole baby?"

Well, I'll tell you. There isn't. There is no room. My midwife said today that she thought the baby was "maybe a little on the big side." Hearing that was like passing a highway sign that warns, "LOW-FLYING AIRCRAFT." Thanks for letting me know, but what am I supposed to do about it? Duck?

All I can do is make room when there is no room. An organ here, a vital bodily function there—just shove over a little bit, everybody. We can do this for a little bit longer.

But how about after the baby is born? You'd think I would have thought of this sooner, but where are we going to put a new baby? Well, in our bed, for quite a while—but what about all those clothes? In a house that is already overflowing with the necessary equipment for keeping ten people looking like someone owns them, where in the world am I going to keep onesies, socks, gowns, receiving blankets, and little jackets, hats, and snowsuits where they will be easy to find, easy to put away, and not trampled underfoot in the galloping pandemonium which is our normal routine?

I responded the same way I do every time I face this particular dilemma: I cried. I couldn't help it. So much of managing a big family is making order out of chaos—not even making things clean, but just making cleaning possible. And despite the relative sanity of our lives these days, facts are facts:

There is just no room.

Eventually, through my tears, I figured out that maybe the sock-and-underwear bin could go over the heating vent. Bibs, aprons, and tablecloths don't actually need their own shelf. The hall chest, which holds broken picture frames, an oddly large collection of grout sealant, and (sigh) the previous baby's baby clothes, could be emptied and moved into the laundry room, in front of a door which will henceforth be considered a wall. And the three perpetually full hampers of clean, unfolded clothing could be wedged on top of the chest, where they will surely be in constant danger of tipping their loads into the toilet, which I won't think about right now.

So, there was room. There was room after all. It's not wonderful, but it works, and it gets the job done. There was a real problem, and I solved it, more or less, without even dying.

That's my plan for Advent this year: making room where there is no room. I have a whole other person who needs space in our house, in our routine, in our lives. What to do? A fresh, breezy room full of spacious shelves and empty closets is not going to attach itself to our house overnight; and I will not become a flawless, holy, worthy receptacle for my savior, the Christ Child, when He comes. I can barely get through a Hail Mary without driving off the road from the sheer distraction, so what can I do to make some room?

Maybe when someone's back hurts, I can resist the temptation to explain about the random fiery paralytic insanity spasms I've been feeling in my back—and just be sympathetic. Maybe when the two-and-a-half-year-old is being unreasonable about her graham crackers, I can search around for a speck of patience for her very real, very silly grief.

I can let my thirteen-year-old win an argument. I can say "Yes" to pancakes with syrup, even though we all just had baths. I can choose not to freak out over a minor irritation at school, and I can say a prayer before answering some creepy troll in my blog's comment box. I can say to my husband, "I'm sorry, I was being crazy. Can we start over?" I can admit that I'm too tired to make pie for the family Thanksgiving get-together, and humbly submit to bringing the mashed potatoes.

When the innkeepers told Joseph that there was no room at the inn, they weren't being jerks—there simply wasn't any space, and that was that. So, as parents have been doing since forever, Mary and Joseph made room where there was no room. My baby is coming, and The Baby is coming, and we have got to make room. For me, this is not the time for major renovations. This is not the time to overhaul everything about my soul. All I need to do is make a little bit of room.

And you could say (*O Magnum Mysterium*)—that it works out well enough.

CHAPTER 3

The Golden Box

Sometimes, it's easy to discern God's will.

If we're faced with the choice of, say, robbing a bank or not robbing a bank, we all know what God wants us to do. The only exception is if we're in an action movie, where the villain has a bomb strapped to our hero and a school bus full of innocent children will die amid flames and wreckage if we don't rob the bank (then the answer is: yes, rob the bank, preferably while shirtless and bleeding).

Most of the time, though, there's no dilemma: follow the law, and you'll be following God's will, QED.

The same is true for the most specific, basic laws of the Church: Go to Mass on Sundays, and you're following God's will. Confess all mortal sins, and you're following God's will. Don't use contraception in your marriage, and you're following God's will, QED.

But when we've already rejected contraception and are trying to figure out whether or not to take the plunge and possibly conceive a child, things get muddier. After all, how could it be God's will that we not have a child? When you phrase it that way, it seems absurd: what, is God going to be mad about having to go to the trouble of making another soul? What, are we going to spend the rest of our lives saying, "Damn, I wish I'd spent those nine months taking classes on making flowers out of gum paste, instead of being pregnant with you, my child?" No, probably not.

All right, so if it's not against God's will for us to have a child, then it must be God's will for us to have a child if we possibly can, right? That seems logical.

Here's an argument you often hear from fertility-nudgers: "What if you and your husband use NFP to avoid pregnancy one month, and that child you didn't conceive is the child who would have cured cancer (or would have grown up to be the pope who reforms the Church, or the president who puts America back on track, or whatever)?"

Yes, what if? It's not easy to refute this view. If we think hard about what we are turning down when we say, "No baby this month!" it's kind of terrifying. When a hamster has a baby hamster, the most it can grow up to be is an adult hamster; so if the parents don't breed, then it's no big deal. But when a human couple conceives a child, that is something unutterably magnificent and irreplaceable (albeit common!). You don't even have to mean it; you don't have to understand it, but you've just made something with a soul that is destined for eternity. This... is a big deal.

How can you possibly say no to this? How could it possibly not be God's will to conceive? I'm going to answer your question in the most annoying way possible: by suggesting that it's a stupid question. Most of my life, I've been halfway imagining that my life is a maze, and at the center of that maze is a pedestal. On the pedestal is a golden box marked (perhaps in Latin) "GOD'S WILL." At the end of my life, I will reach the center of the maze, and I will open up the box and read what's written on a piece of paper inside, and it will say either "Good job!" or "Nope."

And then, presumably, I will spend the rest of eternity either patting myself on the back or weeping and gnashing my teeth. Oh, the suspense!

When I describe the process of following God's will this way, it's pretty easy to see that this is silly: God didn't give us free will as some kind of elaborate game of "gotcha," where we stumble around in the dark while He kicks back and giggles at how silly we all look, bumping into walls. If you think God is like that, then you haven't talked to Him lately. Or looked at a crucifix.

So how *does* God's will work in conjunction with our free will? I don't actually know. But I do know this: it's rare for there to be one single thing which God Wants Us to Do, to the exclusion of all other things.

It's more like when a patient mother, tired of her toddler's indecision, picks out three shirts which she thinks are acceptable, and says, "Okay, it's up to you—which one do you want to wear?" If he stamps his feet and insists on going to the grocery store wearing a torn pillow case, then clearly that's not what his mom wants; but if he chooses the truck shirt, or the bear one, or the one with green stripes, then she will work with him, and find some pants that match. She will let him suffer the tolerable consequences if the bear one is a little too warm for today, because maybe he'll know better next time, and that means his choice was still a valuable one. The truck one and the stripy one also each have their benefits and drawbacks. She will be happy if he chooses either one.

The truth is that there are many different things—even mutually exclusive things—that can be God's will. To switch analogies: when getting to your destination, you might take the scenic route, or the route that gets you the best gas mileage, or the route that takes you through your old hometown, or the shortcut you accidentally discover because the kids were screaming in the back seat and you didn't realize you missed your turn.

Is there such a thing as a wrong road? Yes, of course. Are any of the four I described above wrong roads? No. Are there benefits from taking one that you wouldn't get from taking the others? Yes. But they will all get you there.

So, when we ask ourselves if it's God's will that we have another baby right now, it isn't simply a matter of figuring out whether

God (a) wants you to have a baby, or (b) wants you not to have a baby.

Yes, your choices about fertility heavily involve God's will about bringing new life into the world (and sadly, they sometimes involve realizing that the road you're on is a dark and lonely one, which will lead you to God's will, but without the baby you longed for). But your choices also involve discerning God's will about a number of other things—and that's where the "scenic route vs. best mileage vs. sentimental value vs. blundering around" part comes in.

What are the other things we have to discern, besides "having a baby vs. not having a baby"? We should try to discern if God wants us to learn self-control, or learn trust; if God wants us to focus more on the things around us, or focus more on the long-term view of our life; if God wants us to shower our spouse with extra care and attention for a time, or to stretch our concept of what our marriage is for; if God wants us to have a better understanding of generosity, or a better understanding of prudence; if He wants for us a better acceptance of our own limits, or more sympathy for the struggles of others. And so on.

These are all things which may well be within that golden box marked "God's Will."

One of the dreary misfortunes of living as a lonely Catholic in a world so hostile to babies is that, in our loneliness, we sometimes try to drag God down into our limited view of life: black-and-white, Lord. Just tell me what to do! But He's probably not going to do that.

It's not that God doesn't care about what we do. It's not that the little decisions (and the big ones) of our lives don't matter to Him. They do. After all, He's the one who made our lives this way, full of big and little pleasures and pains.

It's just that what He wants for us is not necessarily tied, ahead of time, to one particular decision—even a decision as large as whether or not to have another child. What He wants, above all, is for us to grow closer to Him. He gives us space (and that's what free will is: working space) to decide what makes sense, and then He says, "All right, kiddo. Let's see what we can do with that."

So, we have our choices within a Catholic understanding of sexuality: we can throw caution to the wind and know as little as possible about when we are likely to conceive; we can chart somewhat, and be willing to take a chance; we can chart strictly, and understand that Sometimes Things Happen, and maybe we'll conceive when we don't especially want to; or we can abstain altogether. We can do any of these things, and conceive when we expect to, or when we don't expect to. We can conceive and then lose a child. We cannot conceive, and receive a child through adoption. We can do any of these things and move away from God; or we can do any of these things and grow closer to God.

That's what's at the heart of it: whether or not we grow closer to God.

So yes, of course there are bad choices. But there are also many, many, many good ones. Free will means having control over our own lives; it doesn't mean having control over God. His will is not tethered to our decisions: He isn't either gleefully or grudgingly willing to follow through with His part of the bargain. His will is larger than that, and we are smaller. And at the same time, we are more precious, much, much more precious to Him: His covenant has less "Okay, fine, be that way" and more "Go ahead, and let's see what we can do!"

God's will is not a checklist of dos and don'ts, but a living, fluid, powerful force that somehow, inconceivably, finds its way into our puny seedling lives, nourishing us like the rain and making us grow and bear fruit.

So, if you insist on seeing life as a maze with a secret answer at the end, I'm going to spoil the surprise for you I already know what's inside that golden box that says "God's Will." There's a little piece of paper, and on it is written your name. That's what He wants: you. How you give yourself to Him is a much, much longer story.

CHAPTER 4

NFP, Providentialism, and Future-You

Among the small fraction of married Catholics who don't contracept, there are two camps: those who space pregnancies by practicing NFP; and providentialists, who may or may not actively pursue pregnancy, but who do nothing to postpone it. Maybe we have respect for Catholics who are in the other camp, and maybe we don't, but we readily identify ourselves as belonging to one or the other.

Well, stop it. Why? First, because it pits us against other Catholics, which makes us anxious to show that we're right; and self-righteous anxiety is never an attitude conducive to discerning God's will. Second, because when we identify our marriage as a providentialist type or an NFP type, it implies that we have to make decisions for our future selves, rather than just making decisions for today.

It reminds me of the debates over home schooling. The decision to home school is so momentous that parents will often load their entire identities into the basket labeled, "We are home schoolers." This way of thinking is satisfying, and helps us to commit fully to our decision when we deal with the day-to-day challenges.

But what happens the next day, when life changes, as life will do, dammit? The basket tips over, and our identities spill out all over the counter, and it's a big mess, right when you're trying to get supper made.

I always advise people considering home schooling to realize that they're not signing up for a twelve-year commitment. They're just making a decision for one year. You give it your all for that one year (and obviously it's a good idea to plan ahead), but don't think too much about "How can I do this for the next twelve years?" Maybe you won't be doing it. Maybe you will move, or get a job, or get sick, or maybe your child will turn out to have special needs you need outside help with, or maybe a new school will open that will do a better job with your kid's talents than you can. Maybe you'll just get tired and need to take a year off.

The point is, you don't know what will happen. This is how life goes, and it's foolish to be such an extremist that you end up eating your words when you find yourself living the life you once railed against. You simply don't know what your future self will have to handle.

The other point is, you don't know what your future self will be able to handle. The future may require entirely different things from what you're managing now. Can't imagine yourself doing those things? Good news: the "now-you" doesn't have to. Your future self will, but your future self will have a whole new tool kit.

Do you imagine that your moral development is at its highest peak right now, and that you know and understand and accept everything you will ever need to know, understand, and accept? Of course not. So if the idea of, for instance, yourself with seven kids freaks you out, that's because you're imagining the now-you with seven kids. If you do eventually have seven kids, you will have changed immensely in the process of having them, one by one.

The same goes for the idea of having to pay attention to a chart: maybe it would feel horrible to you now, but in the future, maybe it will clearly be the right thing to do. So don't even worry about that. Deal with today. Deal with this month, and this year. Don't try and deal now with the things you might have to deal with one day.

Here's a handy example: Here I am with nine kids, with another ten years of likely fertility. For me and my husband, learning how to reach the fabled marriage-building aspects of NFP was a slow and torturous process. You'd think that a couple who practices NFP would grow more and more entrenched in an attitude of control—that learning self-control and prudence would, almost by definition, make a couple less and less willing to accept and be at peace with the unexpected. You'd think a couple using NFP are all about saying no, to each other and to God.

That's how the Younger-Me imagined the Now-Me, fifteen years ago, when I thought about learning to use NFP.

But in fact, the opposite has happened: as we learn self-control, we are both a thousandfold more at peace with the idea of giving up control to God—accepting the unexpected, adapting, being grateful. This is what self-control has taught us. That was unexpected! You never know.

So if you are a providentialist, please be a providentialist right now. Don't assume you know what it does to a marriage to keep charts. Maybe you'll need to do it some day, and you might even like it.

And if you practice NFP and are satisfied that you have good reasons for doing so, don't assume you'll be in this situation forever. Don't think about how Now-You will handle all those potential Then-Kids if you stop charting: just think about what to do now.

Maybe that's why God designed women to be fertile each month, rather than, say, quarterly: so we'd have to keep thinking and thinking about it, revisiting, revising, comparing our desires and needs against our current capabilities. Our challenge is to think about eternity, but to act in the now.

CHAPTER 5

No Petty Virtues

Some time ago, an online discussion of NFP took an interesting turn. I remember it particularly because I got off a pretty good zinger (that's what we Catholic writers do to advance the kingdom of God: we zing people).

The Other Guy's argument went like this: Sure, sure, the Church permits NFP to space out pregnancies in serious circumstances. Because we are a stiff-necked people, she even turns her head while we stretch the definition of "serious." But, if we truly want to follow God, shouldn't we learn to just…let go? Isn't the central lesson of our faith that God will provide for our needs, whether emotional, physical, spiritual, or even financial? NFP (the Other Guy went on) is, more often than not, a crutch which interferes with our radical dependence on God. He is calling us to loosen up that death grip of control and abandon ourselves more generously to His will.

The answer, of course, is that He is calling some people to give up control. To others, the call is entirely different: take charge, be responsible, grow up. Some people are already quite good at living with abandonment, thank you very much, and what God wants from them is a little self-control. It's not even necessarily about having or not having a baby: it's about taking responsibility for your life in general.

Different people, different situations, different lessons to be learned.

And I was gratified when several people said, "Wow, thanks, you're right. I never thought of it that way before." You're welcome, and may God bless you, and may He some day make you as insightful as I am.

At that point, I had it set in my head that family life was a battle of prudence vs. generosity—that some people were called to one, and some to the other. And secretly, I thought that we overly abandoned types had chosen the better part, even in our weakness. I admired people with prudence in much the same way I admired Superman for flying: nice trick, and I wish I could do it—but who really wants to be Superman? Picture the 1940s Man of Steel, with his piercing blue eyes and plastic hair. Is this a guy who could fall in love? How clean he is…and how cold.

I thought of prudence, like temperance, as a dreary virtue. Justice and fortitude are about getting stuff done—but prudence and temperance are all about holding back, clamping down, cutting back, saying no. It's all about the negative: wait, stop, think, don't do it, hold your horses, cut it out. Prudence, I thought, was a virtue, but a petty one.

Or…not. In this season of our life, it seems that another baby is a joy to be postponed for a while yet.

With growing astonishment, I'm discovering that there is no tension between prudence and generosity. Prudence is a kind of generosity. Of course it is! Everything that comes from God over-flows. What is the Promised Land? Not a static place, a spot on the map, but a state of motion, of spilling over—a land *flowing* with milk and honey. And if virtuous behavior imitates God, then how could some virtues be pettier than others?

You can do it wrong. You can exercise self-control with a mean heart, with a bitterness of restraint, or with fear. But that's not true prudence, anymore than it's true fortitude to sit dozing in the back of a bus while someone else steers it through a storm. I did not know how much warmth and love were at the heart of this misunderstood virtue.

When my husband and I realized that God was calling us to work at prudence, I wasn't expecting any emotion at all. I was expecting something utterly dry and mechanical, something contrary to my nature, something foreign to my relationship with my husband.

Instead? It's like one of those dreams where you're wandering around on the top floor of your house, looking for something, something that will satisfy you, something that you need—and what is this? A whole other room. You open the door, and step inside—and there you find what you were looking for: a new kind of satisfaction, a new kind of joy, a whole new vocabulary for expressing love.

There are no petty virtues. Everything that comes from God is a form of love.

CHAPTER 6

Examination of Conscience
for Those Using NFP

Most Catholics use contraception, and that's a fact. Most Catholics don't bother going to confession; and if they did, they wouldn't confess using contraception. But for those of us who follow Church teaching and have sworn off artificial birth control, we're not necessarily home free.

There's a whole new world of sins that open up when we practice NFP—and there ought to be an examination of conscience just for people like us.

An Examination of Conscience for Women

Have I indulged in impure fantasies, such as burning my chart, stuffing my thermometer down the garbage disposal, or sitting down to pee without stopping to analyze the sensation?

Have I ever humiliated my husband by coming out of the confessional and hissing in a stage whisper, "Father says it's all your fault!"

Have I unnecessarily terrified my husband by showing him pictures of the famous "Contact Pregnancy Triplets?"

Have I seriously considered avoiding pregnancy through illicit means such as leaping in front of an oncoming train?

Have I deceived my husband into thinking he must drink castor oil or do humiliating pelvic exercises, knowing full well he's never read the manual and doesn't know any better?

Have I cruelly confused my husband by speaking about how attractive I find a man who is willing to wait?

Have I pretended to be asleep to avoid having sex?

An Examination of Conscience for Men

Have I ever realized that my spouse had fallen asleep in the middle of sex, and pretended not to notice?

Have I ever, for the sake of plausible deniability, pretended I was asleep while I was having sex?

Have I made even the slightest effort to understand what is meant by "tacky"?

Have I made restitution for any sofa arms or door frames that I chewed through while waiting for the green light?

Have I done permanent damage to my children's circadian rhythms by putting them to bed at 3 p.m. because sometimes, dammit, that's going to have to count as the end of the day?

Have I, in the middle of long stretches of abstinence, developed an unseemly interest in wife-shaped objects, such as mannequins, body pillows, or an especially voluptuous ball of pizza dough rising on the counter?

Have I been irreverent when discussing sacred matters, such as mucus? Do I refer to her progesterone cream as "Nutter Butter"? Do I greet her at the end of the day with a loving, "How's your goop?" Does she laugh? If so, is she crying at the same time?

For Both of You

Have I sent death threats to the priest who taught us about NFP? Have I prank called the Vatican? Spread false rumors about the mental acuity of Dr. Billings or Pope Paul VI? Have I spread true rumors about St. Augustine?

Have I ever gone to a seminar about NFP and actually strangled the first teaching couple to use the phrase "honeymoon effect"? How many times? Were they super smug and annoying?

Have I deceitfully kept two sets of charts: one for the instructor, with all acts of intercourse noted; and one for us, with all acts of contrition noted?

Do I prayerfully consider each month whether God is calling us to be generous with our fertility? Or do I only start praying when waiting for that second blue line to appear?

CHAPTER 7

Is It Really Okay to Laugh about Sex?

The other day, someone quoted Ephesians 5 at me:

> But among you there must not be even a hint of sexual immorality, or of any kind of impurity, or of greed, because these are improper for God's holy people. Nor should there be obscenity, foolish talk or coarse joking, which are out of place, but rather thanksgiving. (5:3-4, NIV)

If I understand her properly, she took this to mean that it is wrong to use coarse language in general, and she's probably right about this. Mea culpa. (I also agree with her that it's wrong to be disgusting, to corrupt innocent minds, or to tempt people into sin with words.) But some people also believe that it's always wrong to make jokes about sex—that it's wrong to speak of sex in terms that are not reverent, solemn, and exalted.

This is nuts. It's like telling me to enjoy my meal, but without using my nose. Yeah, taste is of primary concern when we're eating, but we can't just ignore the other cues that normally functioning people pick up when they're eating. Normally functioning people laugh about sex at least some of the time.

I'll go further: if you can't laugh about sex, at least some of the time, then you're doing it wrong. For the standard issue, mildly neurotic, moderately messed up, original-sin-damaged, salvation-seeking, temptation-fighting, humility-seeking, minimally humorous human being, laughing about sex is the sign of good emotional and spiritual health.

I'll go even further: when we're laughing about anything, we're laughing about sex. My theory is that there are two things that make a joke funny: the element of surprise—of being put off balance unexpectedly—and at least a grain of sadness. And that describes sex to a T.

Don't get me wrong! My general attitude toward sex can be reflected in the following statement: "WHOOPEE!" But there's a reason why it's the one thing that everyone has wanted to talk about since forever. I mean, there you are, either having a wonderful time, and/or joyfully contemplating the mysteries of procreation, and then right in the middle of the steaming and the making and the smelling and the baking, tragedy—or at least gravity—pokes through.

Nothing bad happens. Everyone is functioning just fine, and you're having a good time. It's just that…you realize that you're naked. You realize that you're going to die. You realize that you are ridiculous. And you realize that you don't care. This disruption, this intrusion, isn't what spoils the joke of sex: it's what makes it funny.

I'm not just talking about physical intercourse. Human sexuality is about so much more than that. It's the incredibly weird cosmic joke that two things work together only when they're the opposites of each other. It's the baffling irony that innuendo speaks louder than frankness. It's the dance between power and helplessness, and the eye-popping switcheroo when you realize that the balance has profoundly shifted. It's the fearful delight of discovering yet more doors to open. And the blessed defeat when you discover that, sometimes, you'll only get what you need once you give up grasping for it.

These constantly renewed incongruities of sexuality are tragic…and they're funny. As C. S. Lewis says in *The Four Loves*:

I can hardly help regarding it as one of God's jokes, that a passion so soaring, so apparently transcendent as Eros should be thus linked in incongruous symbiosis with a bodily appetite, which, like any other appetite, tactlessly reveals its connections with such mundane factors as weather, health, diet, circulation, and digestion. In Eros at times we seem to be flying; Venus gives us the sudden twitch that reminds us we are really captive balloons. It is a continual demonstration of the truth that we are composite creatures, rational animals, akin on one side to the angels, on the other to tomcats.

It's not just that we may laugh about sex; it's that, at some point, we must. Lewis continues: "It is a bad thing not to be able to take a joke. Worse, not to take a divine joke; made, I grant you, at our expense, but also (who doubts it?) for our endless benefit."

So, how do we tell the difference between just being obscene, getting a little silly, and appreciating a joke that God, with the help of Adam and Eve, designed himself?

Lewis to the rescue again. In *The Screwtape Letters*, he has the master demon teaching his apprentice:

There are some for whom "no passion is as serious as lust" and for whom an indecent story ceases to produce lasciviousness precisely insofar as it becomes funny: there are others in whom laughter and lust are excited at the same moment and by the same things. The first sort joke about sex because it gives rise to many incongruities: the second cultivate incongruities because they afford a pretext to talk about sex.

So if you are wondering if you sin by speaking as you do, you could ask yourself: Where does the humor arise from? What is its aim, and what is its result? Does it make me or another person ugly and perverse? Or is it simply to remind us of the angel/tomcat creatures that we really are?

Does it make us turn away from the light? Or does it acknowledge that all sorts of things are revealed when the lights are on?

PART II

NFP AND THE REST OF THE WORLD

CHAPTER 8

Prudence and Generosity
in Public Conversation

I started learning about NFP sometime in the late 1990s. As I write, it's 2013, and boy oh boy, has the conversation changed. Gradually, more and more Catholics have become willing to talk openly about NFP with each other, and that's been great, overall. But an even more radical change happened when contraception became an issue of American public policy and a constant topic of public debate: suddenly, everyone—practicing Catholics, lapsed Catholics, and non-Catholics—wanted to talk about NFP. Secular news outlets asked practicing Catholics for their views on contraception, rather than following the usual course of noting that the Pope spends his off days kicking back and placing bets on whether the Church's teaching will kill more women through AIDS or childbirth, or just by slowly being crushed to death under a heap of their own ravenous, carbon-hogging offspring.

Anyway, when the mainstream media did interview practicing Catholics, the predictable happened: Catholics got misquoted, and were generally and disastrously misunderstood.

Writer Jennifer Fulwiler was one of these misunderstood Catholics. Her words were twisted badly, and she could understand why. She said on her blog, Conversion Diary:

> [T]he contraceptive worldview is like saying that loaded guns can be used as toys as long as you put blanks in the chamber; in contrast, the Catholic view says that guns

are not toys, and should always be handled with grave respect. Now, to continue with that analogy, in these latest chats about Catholicism and NFP, folks are seeking to understand the Catholic viewpoint by asking which kind of blanks the Church recommends using when playing around with guns.

These kinds of questions are bound to lead to misunderstanding, because they are born from an entirely different understanding of what a gun is in the first place.

When people who are steeped in a Catholic view of sexuality bump up against people who are steeped in a secular view of sexuality, the conversational landscape is about as scenic and lovely as when the mid-Mesozoic supercontinent of Gondwana smashed into Euramerica. Ka-blammo! Not a pastoral scene.

But that's how new worlds get made.

As the public conversation with Catholics began, there was hand-wringing aplenty as true believers contemplated talking about NFP in public. What if we're misunderstood? What if we drive people away, or get laughed at? What if we're too honest, or not honest enough? What if we do it wrong?

The more debate I hear about the proper way to talk about NFP, the more the question reminds me of a sexual relationship (without all the, you know, sex): even when your motives are pure, it can get a little messy. And our motives are not always pure!

Now, some couples live in harmony. They either practice NFP or they don't, and they work in marital accord, sexually and otherwise, their love increasing day to day.

But many others come to marriage wounded, sexually and emotionally. Or they have different temperaments, or they simply need to grow up. As these couples move forward together in their sexual lives, there will be misunderstandings along the way, as they learn how to synthesize a man's and a woman's view of sexuality—to strike a balance between prudence and generosity—to learn how to control themselves without attempting to control God.

Couples like this hold fast to the things they know are true, while allowing their hearts to be changed to accommodate truths they never anticipated.

Couples realize that their own experiences are not necessarily the norm, and learn not to make light of other people's crosses. They make themselves vulnerable. They show courage. They accept that the path forward may not be clear, even when they think they know where they want to arrive.

In the same way, conversations about the Church's view of sexuality are going to be tricky, even for the best-equipped among us. Say, for instance, that I'm a faithful young Catholic who has been brought up with the understanding that sex is a gift, not a right; that babies are a privilege, not a burden; that marriage is for making children and helping us grow in holiness, not for enhancing our portfolios and giving us emotional security and validation.

Confident and righteous, we dive into conversations about human sexuality, armed with the liberating truth.

But then we come head to head with someone whose unfaithful husband refuses to abstain. Or someone with a short life expectancy, who can't admit even the smallest risk of conception. Or someone who already has three severely autistic children. Or someone who doesn't have any extraordinary physical or emotional trials, but who has simply been reared on the world's view of sex, and for whom any amount of abstinence (never mind providentialism) is a mind-blowing impossibility.

Suddenly, just saying the truth as we know it isn't going to do the trick.

In these conversations, just as in the practice of NFP, there will be so many well-meaning attempts to vault ahead to truths that we are not quite ready to live up to.

There will be some surprises along the way, some which bring unexpected blessings, and some that are just ugly setbacks. Some people will hunt for loopholes, and will eventually come around, realizing one more time that the truth is the truth is the truth.

Some people will try to exercise an unseemly control over the conversation, adhering to the truth so rigidly that love is squeezed out of the relationship. And some, eager to be accommodating, become irresponsible and let things slip out of control, until they become unbearably...messy.

Do you see what I'm getting at?

If NFP teaches us to be careful and reverent with our sexuality, then conversations about NFP should teach us to be careful and reverent with the truth. Let's not approach the conversation about the Church's views on sexuality with that fabled contraceptive mentality, holding back what is good and powerful about our Faith and trying to control our interactions with the secular world too rigidly.

At the same time, let's give a thought to prudence: you may think you're being inspired and radical when you open your mouth and leave it up to God to make something good come of it—but maybe some discretion is in order.

In conversation, just as in married love, it's not in our control. Yes, we will be misunderstood when we speak the truth. It just means that it's going to be a long, messy process. The truth will have to be said again and again and again. Alice Von Hildebrand, Christopher West, midwives and theologians, men and women, the continent and the frisky, converts and skeptics: if you know something about NFP, then say it. Don't be afraid.

Want to keep your hands clean? Then you might as well stay home. But if you really want to reach someone's heart, then be prepared for a little bleeding along the way.

CHAPTER 9

You Don't Know

A few years ago, I wrote a lighthearted piece about NFP. Since it's an emotional, sometimes divisive topic, I like to be frivolous about it once in a while. One woman responded with gratitude, and mentioned in passing that she had been married for six years and had no children. Within minutes, another woman leaped in to sneer:

> Well, that kind of says it all, doesn't it. Good news—your marriage may not even be valid, so if you ever want out— just a few pages of paperwork away!

Once I got my breath back, I deleted the comment with a stern warning. One of my favorite hobbies is jumping to conclusions, but even I wouldn't suggest that a perfect stranger's marriage is invalid.

Canon law about marriage is notoriously complex, and not a game for amateurs. Even if the original commenter had said, "I'm a Jehovah's Witness and my third husband is a horse, so I sometimes wonder if my marriage could be invalid," I would refer her question to someone with more experience. I'm telling you, marriage law is complicated.

Besides, the original commenter gave almost no information about herself or her marriage. What went unsaid? Maybe her husband is dying. Maybe she's struggling with bulimia, or maybe she's on lithium or thalidomide, and it isn't safe to conceive. Maybe she's desperate for children, but her husband won't consent; or maybe he's desperate, but her own mother abused her, and she's still working through her terror of being a mother. Or maybe they've had six miscarriages.

Maybe they've been consulting their spiritual director, and he thinks they should wait because of X, Y, or Z, and she doesn't feel like explaining this in the comment box of a total stranger. Who knows? The point is, we don't know; and, that being the case, we have no right to assume anything. Not enough information, too many variables, and nobody asked.

But it's not always so obvious. I remember hearing a group of fat women consoling and encouraging each other in their battle to lose weight. Another woman chimed in, "Oh, I know how it is. I mean, I only have five pounds to lose, but it can be so difficult!"

Jaws dropped. Five pounds? And she thinks she knows how hard it can be? Come on! The rest of the women had fifty or sixty pounds to drop and were enraged by the temerity of this uppity little skinny person. How dare she pretend to understand what they were facing! Five measly pounds! They made sure she understood just how hurtful and discouraging it was for a trim and attractive person like herself to compare her struggle to their own. She didn't know the suffering of the truly obese—the social stigma, the self-loathing, and so on.

She apologized. She retracted. She apologized again. And then the rest of the story came out.

This skinny little lady, it turned out, had given birth to her fourth child a few weeks ago (she is five pounds overweight, let's remember: five). Her husband came into the room where she was getting dressed. She told us how he gazed silently at her body for a moment, and said grimly, "Hmm, looks like it's time for someone to get back to the gym."

Jaws dropped again. What a window into her marriage. We have words for a man like that, but, like Christian Aunt Em, we try not to say them. Suddenly, the skinny little upstart was the one who needed support and consolation.

One more story. This time, the woman in question actually asked for advice. The discussion was about sufficient reasons for postponing another pregnancy. Some of the women looking for guidance had truly difficult cases: was it okay to put off having a baby because your husband's job is in danger? What if you carry a genetic disease, and any child you bear is likely to die young? What if you're already caring for your demented grandfather and your sister's crack baby, your husband is in Afghanistan, and the last four times you got pregnant, it was twins?

What if, asked one woman, you just wanted to lose those last five pounds?

Um, no. No, that wasn't a good enough reason. It was pretty much unanimous. People tried to be kind, but the scorn kept bubbling to the surface. Sorry, but this woman was clearly just being shallow and self-centered. Some women would give their right arm to have another child, and here she was, totally buying in to the modern cult of the body. A loving, Christ-centered marriage based on openness to life and self-donation doesn't have room for a petty little problem like five pounds (why is it always five pounds?) of baby weight. An open-and-shut case. Next!

But a month or two after this conversation, the woman told us what she had just discovered: her husband was cheating on her. It had been going on for years, and the details of his secret life made Hugh Hefner look like a decorous and classy guy. And there she was at home, frantically driving herself on and on with the Stairmaster and the cleansing diets, trying to do what she could to fix what was wrong. She didn't know what was wrong with her marriage. But she did know that having another baby was the wrongest thing in the world right now. She assumed it was her fault.

How shabby we all felt when we remembered our scorn.

Sometimes things really are black and white. Sometimes people really are doing something wrong, and it's our obligation, within specific circumstances, to practice Christian fraternal correction:

> If your brother sins against you, go and tell him his fault, between you and him alone. If he listens to you, you have gained your brother. (Matthew 18:15)

But often there's more to the story. When we are moved to give advice, even if it's solicited, let's remember that the human heart is a strange and tangled jungle of motivations and desires. We keep things hidden even from ourselves, and only God knows who is guilty and who is only wounded.

Come to think of it, what about that first woman I wrote about—the one who responded with guns blazing, so sure that the childless woman was sinning in her marriage? What's her story? Is she happy and contented with her own marriage? Was her unpleasant comment pure, unprovoked aggression—or was she responding to some kind of pain in her own life? Heck, maybe she was just having a terrible day.

God have mercy on us all, and God help us to be merciful to each other.

CHAPTER 10

What Do We Tell Our Kids
(and Ourselves) about Sex?

When my kids reached a certain age, I made a list of basic ideas about sex and relationships that I thought every parent should, in so many words, teach their children. If you don't teach your kids about sex, then someone else will.

But teaching has a horrible way of exposing the teacher. Sometimes, it's not until we try to teach our kids about sex that we realize our own understanding is lacking. If we're having a hard time expressing the Church's teaching on sexuality to our children, it's a great opportunity to ask ourselves whether we've internalized it.

If, instead, we've internalized a worldly view of sex (that it's a right and a necessity, and simultaneously no big deal) or a prudish view of sex (that it's dirty and scary, but a woman's duty), then it will be almost impossible to derive the benefits of NFP—or of a married sexual relationship in general. And it will be a fool's errand to try to teach our kids anything worthwhile or believable, if we don't believe and live these things ourselves.

Here is my list of basic ideas to teach kids. Do you believe these things? Can you teach them to your kids—not only in words, but by example?

We are made to love and to be loved. This is what we are for. God designed us with a desire to show love for other people and to seek love for ourselves. This is not dirty; we are not dirty. Our desire for sex is a desire for love. God designed marriage as a safe and fruitful framework for that love to play out. Outside of marriage, sexual expression is neither safe nor fruitful. (Ask yourself: Do I treat my spouse as someone made to be loved? Do I see myself as someone made to be loved?)

Love is a gift of self. Affection and desire go along with love, but love itself means caring for another person's well-being. If you love someone, you will not involve your beloved in anything that will be bad for him or her. The way you show love to your boyfriend or girlfriend is not the same way you show love to your spouse. (Ask yourself: What have I learned about love since I've been married? How do I treat my spouse differently from when we were dating?)

We speak with our bodies. This means it is also possible to tell lies with our bodies. Being sexually intimate with someone means that you have made vows of fidelity to that person. If you haven't made these vows, you must not act as if you have. (Ask yourself: Have I internalized this connection between what I do and what I mean? Have I made a real effort to learn why the Church forbids certain physical acts, even between married couples?)

Sex is about babies, among other things. Teach them the phrase "unitive and procreative." They should learn enough about a woman's cycle to make the clear connection that the whole system is geared toward procreation. (Ask yourself: Do I think of babies as a risk, as a commodity, as a right? Do I think of babies at all?)

The world lies to you. Have the courage to resist these lies. Kids are proud of not trusting Big Pharma or Big Agra—so remind them not to trust Big Sex (but don't say it like that—that sounds dorky). They are responsible for keeping their heads clear of lies that they learn from books, movies, the Internet, and porn. Tell them what to do: be brave enough to walk out, avert their eyes, or change the topic of conversation. Make sure they know that they are in charge, and that it takes guts to go against the stream. Discuss the chemical effects porn has on the brain, and educate them on how it destroys marriages and the ability to enjoy normal sex. (Ask yourself: Am I content with merely staying technically faithful, or do I work to reject all the lies the world tells me, even about married sex?)

Sex forms bonds, whether the people engaged in it acknowledge this or not—emotional, psychological, spiritual, and scientifically proven chemical bonds. You do not want to form that bond before you're married, because it will hurt like hell to break that bond once it's formed. (Ask yourself: Does my behavior reinforce and sanctify the bond between me and my spouse, or does it weaken it?)

Even if every last person you know is having unmarried sex (and they're not), you don't have to do it. Being chaste doesn't make you a prude or a tease or a weirdo. It may make you different. There are worse things than being different. Catholics should stand out. (Ask yourself: Do I judge our sex life based on what I imagine everyone else is doing? And does my view of sex ever cause me to make sacrifices or to stand out from the crowd? It should!)

Abstinence is a negative; chastity is a positive. Have many discussions about how all people (single, married, religious, heterosexual, and homosexual) are called to chastity, and everyone is called to abstinence, at least occasionally, for various reasons. There are always boundaries in every state of life; and there are always rewards. Licentiousness, however, never leads to happiness, no matter what your state in life. (Ask yourself: What does chastity mean to me as a married person? Do my spouse and I agree? What are we trying to achieve by chaste behavior?)

It's possible to ruin sex for yourself. This is, perhaps, what some abstinence-only educators are trying to get across with the "used tape" exercise: that if you keep forming a bond and then breaking it over and over again, eventually the "tape" is no longer "sticky." Someone who is in this state—who sees sex as a casual, recreational activity with no profound meaning or mystery—is someone who is broken, who is no longer functioning properly. (Ask yourself: Have I considered honestly whether I am sexually wounded? Is my spouse sexually wounded? What can we do to restore ourselves?)

Sex is beautiful and mysterious. No, really. Have you instead found that whatever sexual experience you have had is weird and embarrassing and leaves you feeling crummy and bruised? This is because (a) sex without love is horrible; and (b) sex is a skill that needs to be learned like anything else. So if you've had sex and didn't like it, that doesn't mean that "sex is beautiful" is hogwash (and that abstinence is therefore pointless)—it means that you've been singing the right words to the wrong tune. (Ask yourself: Do I have a cynical view of married sex? If my sex life is not beautiful, what can I change?)

Premarital sex hurts you both, even if you marry the person you had it with. If you never learn self-control before marriage, it will be difficult to learn it afterward. Moreover, sex that comes before commitment makes the entire relationship muddy and messy. One reader shared her teacher's demonstration of a strong relationship: "She built a pyramid of building blocks, with the top block in the relationship being sex. When built correctly, it works well and is great, but when you build the relationship on sex (demonstrator flips pyramid over, it falls apart), it doesn't work because there is no good, strong foundation." (Ask yourself: What am I doing to make my overall relationship strong for any trials to come?)

But all is not lost if you've gone too far. All is never lost. Remind kids that they can go to confession (and make it easy for them to do so, without them having to explain why). Regular family confession is a great practice. Remind them frequently that they can talk to you or to someone you both trust, and that you will never abandon them, even if they disappoint you—and that God will never abandon them, either. It's never too late. If you've fallen, you're in good company. Don't despair. Your past doesn't define you—but your current behavior will affect your future. (Ask yourself: Do I believe that God can heal? How long has it been since my last confession? How long has it been since I've talked to my kids about confession?)

The best lesson about married relationships is the lesson of example. We can say anything we want to our kids, but if we're not living it, they won't believe us. So when we're thinking about teaching our kids, it's a good idea to start with ourselves.

CHAPTER 11

The Worst Possible System,
Except for All the Others

Hey, nice Catholic girls—have you waded into the "sex and relationships" section of any secular women's online magazines lately? You might want to give it a try. Why?

The Catholic echo chamber can skew your perception of how many people agree with you. Constant affirmation (or squabbling over minutiae) dulls your debating skills. And it's healthy and useful to hear opposing arguments straight from the horse's mouth. We also all need to be reminded that even people with beastly ideas aren't The Enemy, and that they and we share a common enemy: Satan. Those of us who know how to pray ought to be doing it for those of us who don't. These are all good reasons to wade out of the shallows of the familiar.

But the main reason I often check out secular blogs and discussion boards? They make me realize how good I've got it. This is especially true in matters of sex, and most especially in the contraception vs. NFP debate.

No matter how firmly we believe that sex is intended for procreation and for fostering the union between husband and wife, no matter how well we've memorized the concept of the gift of sexual union mirroring the perfect caritas of the Holy Trinity— well, most of us are not entirely deaf to the song the secular world is singing. Those ideas do penetrate.

Which ideas? The myth that most of the developed world enjoys sex as a lifelong, carefree romp. That, requiring only a consenting partner, most people can have sex whenever they want to, whenever the mood hits them, however they damn well feel like it, and there is no problem. In the contraceptive myth, women are never put at a disadvantage as long as they're exercising choice; and while sex may occasionally be a little silly or disappointing, it's never something you can't shrug off. If your sex life doesn't resemble your favorite romantic comedy, it's just a matter of going back to the clinic for another tidy solution that works better for you.

Whereas here we are, married, for crying out loud, and we're chewing the mattress to bits in frustration.

We know that the contraceptive lifestyle is immoral. But it sounds *so easy*.

The truth is, of course, that it isn't. This side of Eden, nothing important is easy. Sooner or later, sex is going to call for some kind of self-sacrifice. Sex is going to cause complications, and this is true whether you're going au naturel, charting feverishly, or cramming your body with every spring, cork, dam, plug, sponge, and toxin you can lay your hands on.

So if you, O faithful Catholic spouse, are experiencing some disenchantment—if you find yourself wishing that you could, for once, just ditch these awkward, inharmonious shenanigans called "the fertile years"—if you wish you could just take a break and enjoy some of that easy-peasy secular sex for a change—then think again. Because there is no such thing.

Don't read the talking points about contraception from mainstream medical Web sites or Planned Parenthood; and don't read dire, hand-wringing what's-the-world-coming-to posts by prolifers. Instead, read chatty blogs and unfiltered comments from actual people who contracept as a way of life, speaking frankly to like-minded people. First, prepare yourself for some nasty language and ugly ideas, but then *tolle et lege,* and start feeling sane and normal again.

Google "discussion forum" + whatever form of contraception or sterilization you think would solve your problems. Read all the comments.

Google "birth control didn't work."

Google "vaginal ring" and "stank."

Google "birth control makes me crazy."

Google "contraception" + "relationship problems."

Google "hormonal birth control" + "lost sex drive."

Google the name of the contraception you've heard makes life wonderful + "almost killed me" or "lawsuit" or "horror stories" or "fatality."

And read articles in hip, edgy, in-your-face magazines for women. Read any article, positive or negative, having to do with birth control, and then read the comments. See what happens when one woman says that she had a bad experience: see whether other women stick up for her, or if they keep on defensively trotting out the party line that birth control is necessary, birth control is inevitable, birth control (and bleeding, and losing hair, and chronic bacterial infections, and depression, and cramping, and nausea, and severe mood swings, and weight gain, and loss of sex drive, and memory loss, and vaginal cysts, and blood clots, and and and) is something that empowers women—something that makes normal life possible.

Read up, and ask yourself if it seems normal and rational for so many women to be suffering this way. Ask yourself how it would help your relationship to be going through these things, and to have your husband watching it happen. Remind yourself that, even if you're suffering with NFP, at least you're being honest: at least you're dealing with the real effects of real sex, head-on.

You have chosen the better part.

The point of reading about the other side is not to scare yourself straight, and the point is not to look down on anybody. The point is to remind yourself that, when it comes to facing fertility, all God's children got angst. Take it from women on the front lines: there is no easy way to sidestep fertility. The only way to make sex simple is to opt out entirely.

Are you having a hard time with NFP? Well, that is what sex is like sometimes, especially if you've allowed your conscience to develop in any meaningful way. It's not a Catholic problem, it's a fallen world problem. Anyone who says differently is selling something that is likely to be the object of a class action medical lawsuit in ten years.

NFP: it's the worst possible system, except for all the others.

CHAPTER 12

Ask Your Doctor If Irreversible
Mutilation Is Right for You!

You'd think a doctor would know what a uterus is for.
You'd think that somewhere, in all those years of medical school, there'd be a class or two about how to care for regular old women—women who do womanly things, like getting pregnant, giving birth, charting cycles, and not wanting to be poisoned or mutilated. But as any NFP-using grand multipara knows, the medical world considers such a woman baffling, backward, diseased, and nuts.

As if it weren't exciting enough to raise a family, we procreators also find ourselves having to fight off the culture of death right when we're at our most vulnerable: pregnant, or newly postpartum, or just literally with our pants down.

The typical comments from secular doctors range from the annoying ("Tell me when you get tired of the rhythm method, and we'll write you up a script for something that works") to the ignorant ("But what if your cycles aren't always 28 days?") to the criminally nasty: A woman I know went to her OB/GYN, grieving after losing yet another baby. "You know," sniped the receptionist, "You should get some real birth control—can't just keep counting on having all these miscarriages!" Why such a malignant harpy worked at a women's health center, I'll never know; but she should have been fired, then horsewhipped, then rehired, horsewhipped, and fired again.

I'll never forget the send-off I got after giving birth to my first child. As my husband packed my bags, I crouched on the hospital bed like a cavewoman at bay, clutching my wrinkly little newborn and yelling at the doctor, "I know what's in that little paper bag! You might as well throw it away, because I told you and I told you, we will not be using your damn condoms!" But policy was policy, and she was required to leave them.

A few years and three babies later, I was on the phone answering a survey. The caller wanted to know which type of birth control I used (I think it was a push poll designed to show that the government should spend more money sterilizing poor people). When I said that I didn't use birth control, he wanted to know why not. So I hollered, "Because I'm not afraid of babies, like some people!" and slammed down the phone.

For the record, I don't yell as much as I used to. Also for the record, I see now why I was so belligerent: it was because, despite what I said, I was afraid of babies. Terrified, to be exact. I was utterly surrounded by them, and the only plan I could come up with was to make it look like I had gotten there on purpose.

Today, I've more or less made peace with my galumphing fecundity, and hardly get rattled when someone suggests that I try and fix what ain't broke. I know that my winsome children are something more than symptoms of the embarrassing disease called fertility. People who think otherwise are to be pitied, not yelled at. Margaret Sanger, where is thy sting? You're dead, but I'm either pregnant or likely to get that way. I win!

But sometimes it's not the "better living through sterilization" routine that catches me off guard—it's an excess of natural thinking. I once found a midwife who, to my initial delight, was pleased to hear that I use NFP. She was the type who mucked about the hospital in wooden clogs and kept her portable Doppler device in a woven satchel from Guatemala. She dabbled in homeopathy, and encouraged water births and various tinctures of this and that for what ails you (and when you're pregnant, everything ails you). So I felt safe with her, and complained a bit about the trials of charting postpartum. She must have felt safe with me, too, because she recommended doing what she and her husband do to avoid a pregnancy.

Ahem. Without going into specifics, let's just say I was glad to know that the Church forbids this practice, and that it doesn't work very well—because it's gross. That's actually what I blurted out to her: "I don't think I do laundry often enough to try that at home!" I wonder if there's a homeopathic treatment to erase your memory of traumatic information. There's definitely such a thing as too much nature.

But the strangest experience of all is to be under the care of a doctor who is caught halfway between naturopathy and what I think of as "sexnology": she loves chatting about hypnotherapy and raspberry leaf tea and probably keeps a few encapsulated placentas in her carry-on bag, in case of emergency. But she's still a modern doctor, and suckled at the toxic breast of radical feminism. And she knows who writes her paychecks, too (hint: it's not the Vatican).

Once I was under the care of one such curious medical hybrid. I found myself waiting for a good half-hour in her tiny exam room, which was decorated in high contraceptive style: charts and posters everywhere, comparing the benefits of various hormones, devices, and procedures—and sheaves of pamphlets with that ubiquitous young Hispanic model, her long-lashed eyes slewed off to the side as she contemplates Choice. And, of course, the countertop was littered with rubbery little anatomical models, showing exactly where, in a woman's pink parts, the spring, plug, clothespin, or cork would be inserted.

Finally, the doctor arrived, and we had a standard prenatal visit. I measured fine, my numbers looked good, and we enjoyed listening to the little one's heartbeat, like the footfalls of a galloping mouse. All was well. Finally, she asked if I had any questions.

Well, nothing urgent, but I did have one problem: I'd been sweating like a pig throughout the pregnancy, and my normal antiperspirant just wasn't doing the job anymore. Did she, I asked, have another antiperspirant to recommend?

I swear to you, this happened: "Oh," she gasped. "Oh, oh no! Sweating is natural—it's something the body is designed to do. We wouldn't want to interfere with a normal, natural process like that!" And, sweeping aside some fallopian tubes that were cluttering up the place, she made a note about where to shop for dress shields.

PART III

———

NFP IN THE
TRENCHES

CHAPTER 13

Why NFP Hurts

Are you skeptical about the difficulties of NFP? Are you and your spouse actually kind of fine with abstaining when you need to? Or are you yourself fine with it, and do you roll your eyes when your spouse complains? When someone writes a piece called, "Why NFP hurts," do you groan and say, "Oh, please! No more whining about NFP! So you have to keep your knickers up for a week or so—so what? No one ever died from not having sex."

Well, you're right. No one ever died from not having sex. Sure, abstaining while married is hard. Abstaining indefinitely, while you figure out what the heck your chart is trying to say, is even harder.

But the painful part, and the part that people usually refer to when they complain about NFP, is the part that somehow never gets explained in all the flowery pamphlets extolling the closeness, the respect, the swooning anticipation that periodic abstinence promotes. The hard part comes when you're figuring out how to abstain—what to do, what not to do, how to speak about it, how to understand what your spouse is going through. The hard part is learning how to avoid being driven apart by this "unitive" gift from God.

This is where the misunderstandings come in, and where even loving couples begin to hurt each other: in the learning stage. And the learning stage can take years. There is no pain like being hurt by someone you love, unless it's the pain of knowing you're hurting the one you love, and you don't know how to stop. God wants you to be good to your spouse, but it seems like there's nothing godly you can offer.

NFP is like a lens. The man is on one side, and the woman is on the other. They can see each other through it—but sometimes the image is distorted, ugly, mangled. The woman might say: "I don't think we should do such and such if we can't follow through tonight"—but if the lens is tilted the wrong way, all her husband hears is, "Stay away from me, perv."

Or her husband can say, "I just miss being close to you!" but it comes out, "I liked the sex, but the rest of our relationship is pointless."

The woman pleads, "I can't handle another pregnancy right now," but it comes out, "You might as well keep it zipped up until we're in the nursing home."

Or the man mumbles, "We're abstaining so much, maybe we should think about having another baby," and it comes out, "The hell with you and your complaining, as long as I get what I want."

You start out trying to please God, and you end up shredding your marriage. It's not that you're unwilling to follow the Church—it's just that no one warned you that obedience could be this awful.

The lens of NFP can concentrate the mild heat of a minor character flaw or marital quibble into a searing, unbearable intensity. A man who values privacy, for instance, may become a monster of silence, cruelly wounding his wife every month; while a woman somewhat prone to scruples may begin to fear and despise her husband's natural physicality. Or a man who is slightly insecure can mistake his wife's caution for distaste, and begin to feel guilt over his healthy desires—and then feel rage that he is made to feel guilty. Or a woman who is slightly selfish can nourish resentment in her heart over the unequal burden of being keeper of the chart—and then feel used when they finally do come together. A few months of these marital distortions, and you may be ready to chuck it all—just head to the nearest surgeon, fix things up, and go to confession later.

It's common to go through this, no matter what the hearts-'n'-flowers training manual says. Don't despair. If NFP brings you suffering, it doesn't mean your marriage is a failure, or that you're invincibly worldly or immature. It just means that love, like all the best things in life, is complicated. So complicated.

So if NFP is a lens, maybe it's a flexible one. Twist the lens into another shape, and the wife can groan, "I don't completely know what's going on in this cycle"—and it comes out: "You are a good husband, a real, strong man who makes me feel safe, even when I have bad news." This is what a man at his best wants to hear (even more than he wants to hear, "Yes, dear, anything you say").

And the husband can eagerly ask, "Do you think we'll be on for this weekend?"—and it might come out, "You're so beautiful that it's hard to wait, but what I want most of all is to make you happy." This is what a woman at her best wants to hear (even more than she wants to hear, "You're so sexy, I can't stop myself").

NFP first gave me and my husband several years of incredible pain, and then several years of a strange and unexpected joy. We've finally learned that NFP can take a nascent impulse toward love and magnify it into something profound and joyful, something that will make your heart overflow, something new. The system hasn't changed, of course. We have changed.

We thought we needed to bend the method, twist that lens to suit our needs. But it turned out that it wasn't the lens that needed to change shape. In order to make it work—not only to help us plan pregnancies, but to help us to turn small gestures of affection into strong and abiding love—we needed to leave that lens where it was, but stand in a different spot. Both of us.

How do you make the shift?

I'm sorry I have nothing radical to report, just more of the same old Catholic advice: prayer, persistence, frequent confession, and, once you're done cursing and crying and chewing your nails, remembering to laugh. You've tried fighting, you've tried whining, you've tried cheating, stonewalling, cajoling, and demanding, and you've tried hiding. But here's what NFP tells us: try sympathy.

It doesn't sound like much, but it's so hard. A husband must have sympathy for his wife; a wife must have sympathy for her husband. Sympathy for what? For someone else's pain, for something foreign to you, a suffering you do not personally feel.

Sympathy comes only through understanding, and understanding comes only through love. Most married couples do love each other. So you have the first ingredient, anyway. Hold on to that.

But understand that love is not something you have—love is something you use.

To you battle-scarred matriarchs and patriarchs who roll your eyes at the struggles of a young couple just starting out with a shiny new chart: why don't you have some sympathy, too? Have some sympathy for people who struggle, and never make them feel that their suffering is trivial.

Hooray for the couples who handle NFP with grace and poise. Hooray for the ones who have managed to steer into one of those swift currents of grace, which pulls them along with some effort to stay on course, but with no real struggle. Hooray for them, and may their good luck continue.

But my real admiration goes to the couples who hate NFP, hate what it does to their marriage, hate the way they are treated by their self-righteous fellow Catholics. I admire the ones who hate everything about NFP—but who pick themselves up and try it again next month, because somewhere in the midst of the suffering is an unwilling groan, "Thy will be done."

I admire the couples who keep coming back for more until they finally get it right: the ones who make themselves lie down on that altar again until NFP becomes—is it too much to say?—an unbloody sacrifice. Because that's when the real benefits come: once you've hung around for the horrible part, and died to yourself, and risen again. It happens each month. But it also happens more profoundly over the life of a marriage.

The worst part of NFP is what gives it its strength: it's a chance to set aside your own pain and to bind up the wounds of the one you love. It gives you the chance to assist in someone else's sacrifice —whether that other person is your husband or wife, or another couple looking for some understanding, sympathy, and hope.

What NFP teaches us is that a cross is a cross, even if you're not the one carrying it.

CHAPTER 14

How to Ruin Your Marriage with NFP

Couples who use NFP have an incredibly low rate of divorce, and many couples have reported that using NFP to space pregnancies has led to an increase of grace, happiness, and intimacy in their marriage.

Sound too good to be true? It sure is! Oh, using NFP can strengthen your marriage, but that doesn't happen automatically. In fact, there are tons of easy and excellent ways to ruin your marriage while using NFP to postpone pregnancy. If you're interested in sharing many miserable years with your spouse, here's your action plan:

1. Men, make your wife feel either "useful" or "useless," depending on her current fertility. For instance, if you agree to postpone a pregnancy, launch a relentless campaign to make her have sex anyway, or to satisfy you in illicit ways. You don't have to use physical force; there are plenty of other ways to exert pressure.

   You can be nasty or sullen toward the whole family when you're abstaining.

   You can always make her be the one who says "stop," as if she's the owner of sex, and you're the beggar. This should make you both resentful.

   In the name of chastity, you can shun her when she's fertile, so that, by the time you get the green light, she will be so hurt by your attitude that your sex life will be abysmal. You can turn to porn and masturbation, to make her feel like sex with her is your preference, but there are many close seconds.

And when you do have sex, make sure she gives you what you've got coming. You deserve it, for waiting this long.

CAUTION: If you consider her pleasure as important as yours when you do have sex, you might have to ask awkward questions about what works and what doesn't, and this will lead to better sex for both of you. If you let her know that you desire her madly, but care for her so tenderly that you are willing to wait—if you clearly enjoy being with her even when she has clothes on—she will swoon. DO NOT DO THIS.

2. When she is pregnant, make sure she knows it's her problem, not yours. Ditto for all aspects of child care. This tactic is versatile: if you're more practical than she is, you can shame her for falling for irrelevant, outdated pieties; or if you're holier than she is, you can shame her for not being more open to life. Either way, it's all her fault. This is probably what St. Joseph did.

CAUTION: If you spend time changing diapers, washing dishes, playing with the kids, and listening closely when she explains what her days are like—if you care about what worries her, and ask how you can relieve her workload—she will think of you as a real man, and may even experience less anxiety about conceiving in the future. DO NOT DO THIS.

3. Women, remember that sex is important to men because men are pigs. They actually receive love primarily through

physical means, if you can imagine such a thing. They are so foul and immature that they actually feel lonely and wounded when they don't receive physical affection.

Make them feel guilty every time they touch you. Be cold and scrupulous.

When abstaining, act like an Amish schoolgirl, as if married chastity is the same as unmarried chastity.

When you do have sex, choose that day to scrub the wallpaper or clean out the attic, so you will be exhausted by the time your husband comes home.

Remember that holy women don't enjoy carnal things, so make no effort to become skillful in bed. Also, holy men only care about spiritual things, so make no effort to be physically attractive.

Do not learn his tastes; do not communicate your tastes. Remember that the whole thing is just nasty, and basically a joke on women.

CAUTION: If, through trial and error, perseverance and communication, and lots of trips to confession, you do work out how to be physical enough to communicate love, but not so physical that you're making things worse, your affection will deepen, and your sex life will probably improve. Abstinence will become more manageable, or at least more interesting. DO NOT DO THIS.

4. Register your dissatisfaction with NFP by charting sloppily. If you resent charting and do it poorly, your confidence will be shot, your guilt/resentment quotients will increase, and the next time you are faced with a serious need to avoid pregnancy, you will likely have a nervous

breakdown. Your husband will be too terrified to touch you. Voila! No pregnancy.

CAUTION: Charting conscientiously shows your husband that you're interested in finding as many available days as possible, because you like sex, and because you like him. DO NOT DO THIS.

Men and women:

5. Constantly compare yourself to other families you see at Mass, even though you're seeing them at their best and comparing it to your secret, interior worst. Also, when a stranger makes a comment on Facebook, take that very seriously; but disregard everything you know about your actual family, your temperament, your spouse's temperament, your history, your financial situation, your children's needs, your emotional state, and your relationship with God.

   CAUTION: Making prayerful decisions about your individual, unique marriage can lead to maturity, increases in self-control and self-knowledge in all areas, healthy confidence, compassion toward other people, and a greater understanding of how free will operates in cooperation with God's will. DO NOT DO THIS.

6. Constantly surround yourself with secular influences, lest you hear firsthand the Church's teachings about human sexuality. Saturate yourself with the idea that sex is a right, and that NFP is the culprit that deprives you of your rights. Bitterly grumble that, if NFP is so "natural," it ought to be easy and pleasant. Never stop and think that truly "natural" things are things which make you

consider their true nature. Never dwell on the true nature of sex.

CAUTION: Remember, Christ told us to take up our cross, and promised that suffering leads to salvation if we embrace it willingly. DO NOT DO THIS.

7. Do not talk about it with your spouse. Assume that, as in all things, men and women see life in exactly the same way. There is no possible way you are misunderstanding each other's motives, attitudes, or behavior.

CAUTION: Talking about it may help you to understand your spouse better in general, not just in the bedroom, and may lead to enlightenment and compassion. DO NOT DO THIS.

8. Do not laugh about it. Sex is holy, and holy things are never funny. Ever. Even when you're naked.

CAUTION: Laughter leads to closeness and relieves anxiety. DO NOT DO THIS.

9. Above all, never pray about it. God does not want to hear about yucky, embarrassing stuff like that. Ideally, you should suffer all the unpleasant consequences of original sin without enjoying any of the benefits of the Incarnation. Remind yourself frequently that the main thing God does is say "NO," and that you can unerringly anticipate everything God has in store for your life.

CAUTION: Remember, sex is a powerful thing which can, in any marriage, become cramped, dark, and full of pain. If you pray about sex to God, who invented sex, He may shed light on it for you. He may transform your sexual relationship with your spouse into a source of joy, which may then transform your life, whether you're abstaining or not. DO NOT DO THIS.

****

Well, there you have it. Using these simple guidelines, you can do a bad job of avoiding pregnancy and wreak horrible damage on your relationship.

The best part? You can just blame NFP.

CHAPTER 15

The Tangled Chain:
Pursuing Chastity in Marriage

Hey, you made it! Here you are on the other side of ovulation, and you can finally let loose. You can actually have sex. You don't have to worry about going too far, because you have arrived. Right?

Yeah, pretty much! But most couples, at some point, will ask themselves, "Are Catholics really allowed to do such and such?"

Some of this hesitance is due to plain old prudery or a genuinely un-Catholic understanding of the body: some people are terrified of pleasure in general, even though sexual pleasure is a gift from God.

Some of this concern is a natural reaction for people who've struggled mightily to abstain until marriage. It's hard to flip that switch, to go from "Danger, danger, don't even get near that," to "Whoopeee!" just because you have a wedding ring on.

And a huge amount of doubt is due to the onslaught of genuinely perverted material that we are exposed to when we step out the door. Many of us have pasts we're not proud of. Most of us have images and ideas which are bound up with passion and desire. It's not easy to figure out what belongs in our marriages and what doesn't.

Many of us are kind of nervous about sex.

Some people try to clear up all of this nervousness with a reassuring sound bite: "As long as his good stuff ends up in her good stuff, you're okay." In other words, any sexual behavior is acceptable as long as the husband eventually ejaculates inside his wife's vagina, and anything before or after that is fine. (Also: a woman may have an orgasm before, during or after intercourse, as long as it's in the same "session.")

This is true, but stupid. Or it's true, but depressingly limited. It has everything to do with biology, little to do with chastity, and almost nothing to do with love—which is always a bad idea when you're having sex with your beloved.

So, unsatisfied with this sound-bite theology, I asked a priest if this was true—can you really do anything, as long as it turns out okay? He said, "Yes...as long as it doesn't end up being all about that thing." And this idea, although it sounds just as simple, has been a much more fruitful line of thinking for me. Because if you're trying to make sure you're not making sex "all about that one thing," then you must be hoping to make it all about something else, right?

So what are we trying to make it about? In other words, what is chaste behavior, besides refraining from doing things you know are wrong?

Chaste behavior is untangled behavior. Chaste behavior is behavior that restores us to our true selves, so that we can be united with our spouses in a way that is fruitful (whether we're conceiving a child or not). And chaste behavior is rooted in freedom. Not licentiousness, but true freedom. Freedom means being untangled.

When we make love with our spouses, we're becoming one, physically; and we're working (over the course of a marriage) toward becoming one spiritually. It's not enough to learn how to get along without fighting. What you want—what you want it to be all about—is to learn how to function as a single entity, because that, as a married couple, is what you are now.

But there is nothing in the world more complicated than a single human being, and now, in marriage, we have two of them… and they're supposed to come together in harmony? No wonder it's complicated. No wonder people are worried and confused. And no wonder people aren't thrilled at the idea of pursuing chastity within marriage. Hell, we're married. We're faithful to each other, and we're not using contraception—what more can God possibly want from us? And isn't it totally going to ruin everything if we start getting all chaste all the time?

A woman looks at her husband and somehow fails to think, "If only you could be more like St. Paul!" A man walks by a Victoria's Secret storefront and doesn't immediately think, "Gee, I can't wait to get home so my wife can strive to make me more like Christ tonight." We want, in a theoretical way, to be holy, but perhaps we are afraid that holiness in sex will be…well, boring.

Many people are terrified that, if they become holier, they will be giving up everything that makes life good.

But chastity doesn't mean having sex with a halo on. While it's true that the sexual union of a man and a woman reflects, in a small way, the eternal love between the Persons of the Trinity, and that the potential for procreativity is a profound homage to the infinite creativity of God…it's also true that, well, you're not God. You're just this dude and this chick, and not every act you perform together has to carry an entire freight of existential significance that elevates your souls. Panting and sweating is allowed. Like the song says, "Praise the Lord and swing into position, and we'll all stay free."

So don't worry if you don't feel all spiritual when you're having sex. Sex is spiritually significant whether we like it, or realize it, or not. The significance is there, whether we do it right or not. The significance is there, which is why it's worth doing right. We should pursue chastity, and not just be content with getting his good stuff into her good stuff.

Let's return to the notion that freedom means being untangled. Think of a chain with a clasp at each end, designed to attach one to the other. Say that someone gave it to you as a wedding present, but by the time you get to your brand new apartment and open your jewelry case, the chain is all snarled up. You can probably get the ends to connect to each other, and in theory, they will be functioning properly—but what would the purpose be? It won't look good when you wear it, and it's clearly not at all useful. It's still a golden chain, and it still technically works, but it's not doing what it's supposed to do.

If you want that chain to serve its function, you have to take the time to unsnarl it. Each end has to be carefully worked around each other, in and around and over and under and through. This takes patience and time, and sometimes all the maneuvering makes things worse temporarily. This is what the process is like, when you're sorting out what sort of things do and do not belong in your sexual relationship.

And here's the real revelation: when you finally do unsnarl the thing, the two ends are actually further apart than they were when they were in a tangled mess.

Further apart in what sense? Well, a husband and wife who have learned the meaning of chastity may find that they are learning all sorts of things about how men and women are different from each other—not only biologically and emotionally, but in their natures.

And, once they are untangled, they may find themselves enjoying each other's differences, rather than chafing over them. My husband and I have untangled many of our snarls, and we have found ourselves more distinct from each other—and more ourselves.

So there you are, a married couple, one on one side, one on the other, wonderfully distinct, with a firm, clear role, all untangled—and yet there is this space between you. No snarls, no tangles—so what's the next step?

Well, duh. Now you can join together.

Think of how satisfying it is to put that necklace on for the first time after you've gone through the process of de-snarling. You go, "Ah-hah, now we have something here." You have truly regained something.

What kind of things? I, for one, have gained (at least some days!) the patience and maturity to take on certain wifely or motherly roles that don't come easily and naturally to me, because I know that this is what makes our relationship work better. I understand that making these concessions doesn't mean that I'm losing my identity. I see clearly that moving forward in my faith doesn't guarantee that life will get easier—but I still (well, most of the time) want to move forward.

I can now admit that, as a woman, I want certain things, things that I used to think of as signs of weakness, or as trite or clichéd. I now have the courage to speak my desires without worrying that I will be turned down or laughed at or misunderstood; and I have the self-confidence to deal with it when all my desires are not fulfilled. I have the strength to ask questions whose answers I might not like.

I can see my fertility as a gift that I need help caring for, not as a burden that I ought to be compensated for. And even as my body gets older and less objectively appealing, I can see it more and more as a gift that I am glad to share with my husband. Even as we become more skilled at the practice of sex, we worry less over the occasional dud. And we worry less about being sexy, and learn how to relax and enjoy—and how to give joy.

Most of all, becoming untangled meant learning to let go of struggles for fairness and equality, and learning to look instead for unity and harmony. I never thought I'd get there. I never would have, if we'd been satisfied to remain tangled.

As we work through our tangles, I discover more and more what it means to be a woman, and I think I understand better what it means for my husband to be a man—even in matters which don't have to do with sex at all.

So when I speak about untangling sexual snarls, what sort of things do I mean? Well, there are some that we probably actually want to untangle: not feeling physically or emotionally satisfied, for instance; or knowing that how we deal with each other is causing fights and unhappiness. Usually, at least one spouse is pretty motivated to work out these tangles.

But what about other things—things which are deeply enmeshed in our relationship, and which we may suspect are not in keeping with a Catholic marriage, but which we simply don't want to get rid of? Attitudes, specific practices—things you don't want to give up, because they turn you on? Things which don't preclude his good stuff from getting in her good stuff—but which don't sit right?

You will benefit from untangling these things, too—but how do you begin?

It may be helpful to ask yourself, "Where does this desire come from? What does it tap into?" Is it related to something that is unseemly or unhelpful, like self-hatred or a desire to hurt? Or is it something that you saw somewhere and can't get out of your head? These are things that may technically, legalistically be permissible, but they are not helpful, and they may prevent you from growing closer to your spouse. They may prevent you, ultimately, from becoming who you yourself ought to be.

First, you can always just pray for God to take a certain desire away from you. "Lord, if this is no good, please take it away!" Sometimes He does that. It never hurts to be specific!

Another way to work at unsnarling a tangled sex life is to look at everything besides sex. Work on your self-loathing, and you may discover other worrisome things falling away. Work on your kindness, and you may discover you're more inventive in the bedroom.

And if there's something that you're just plain not sure about, don't worry about figuring out once and for all if it's kosher or not. Just take a break from it. Do without. Keep it simple, and see how it goes for both of you.

Above all, talk about it with each other. Silence is where problems grow.

And be patient with yourself and with your spouse. Sexual love is something you have to learn. The longer you are married, desire and affection should become more and more enmeshed with each other—and the longer you are married, the easier it will be to identify when you are truly expressing love, and when you are simply looking for gratification or relief.

So, in a way, that irritating sound bite about his good stuff and her good stuff is actually not too far off base. But you might need some time and work to broaden your definition of what "good stuff" actually is. It's about more than genitals!

Sex is about joining together what is good in you and good in your spouse—and about making sure that you end up joined together not only physically, but spiritually, and not only in bed, but in every aspect of your marriage.

When we decide to get married, we have to make sure, first, that we are free to do so: that there are no encumbrances that would prevent us from joining together freely. This work continues after the wedding. Marriage is the constant work of freeing ourselves, and untangling ourselves, so that we can learn, like two ends of a golden chain, to come together.

CHAPTER 16

Groping Toward Chastity

First, let's get something straight: chastity is not the same as celibacy. Single people must be celibate; the religious vow to be celibate; and very occasionally, a married couple must be celibate. But every single human being is called to chastity, all the time.

Chastity looks different depending on your state in life, and chastity within marriage looks different at different times, during the course of a marriage—at least, the specific behavior looks different.

My goal here—and my goal within my marriage, as a matter of fact—is to arrive at the point where the specifics may look different, but it's obvious that the overarching attitude toward sexuality is the same. Abstinence is a negative concept, but chastity is a positive; and, whatever else you might think about the Church, you have to admit she's consistent.

It's hard to think of chastity as a positive when you're married and abstaining. You want to have sex, and feel like you ought to be able to have sex, because you're married—but you can't. And it's hard to think of it that way if you're struggling with some particular behavior—something that one or both of you enjoys, but which makes you wonder, "Is it okay for Catholics to do this?"

There are, of course, things which are never permissible for a married couple, whether they're abstaining or not. Pornography, whether pictures or video or books, is never permissible, even if the couple consumes it together. It is dehumanizing to the person portrayed, and it is dehumanizing for the person consuming it:

just like contraception, it separates sexual stimulation from the act of intercourse. It may lead to more heat in the short term, but in the long term, pornography kills love.

Another non-gray area: if they're not going to have intercourse, neither the man nor the woman should have, try to have, or try to give their spouse an orgasm. And no fair playing the "I had no idea that would happen!" game unless you're brand new at sex. Accidents happen, but not everything that happens is an accident, so we have to be honest with ourselves.

So some behaviors are clearly out. But when a couple is abstaining, they may find themselves in a shady middle ground of sexual behavior. We do not turn into nonsexual beings as soon as intercourse is off the table. And we can't always definitively say, "Behavior X is a sign of affection, but behavior Y is a sign of lust." Affection and desire are not always neatly divided, and that's a good thing! Especially if the abstinence is prolonged, a husband and wife may find themselves wanting to express love in physical ways, either out of simple desire, or out of a desire to make their spouse feel cared for, or just out of genuine affection.

The general rule is: you're not supposed to go seeking after sexual pleasure when you know you're not going to consummate it. Deciding where to draw the line is a little trickier.

It is strangely difficult to get straight information about what is and is not appropriate sexual behavior within a marriage. We should realize that the standards for married couples are different from the standards for the single or engaged couple; but beyond that, there's not a lot of reliable, objective information.

I'm starting to think that this dearth of information is a feature, not a bug—that couples need to grow into chastity through their own plan, and that having someone else set down ground rules would inhibit development, not encourage it.

So how do you encourage growth? The first thing to get straight is what's prudent and what's not: you have to be honest with yourself and with each other. "If we do such and such, which may or may not be okay, are we going to go too far into something that's definitely not okay?" These behaviors vary from couple to couple: one couple might not even be able to enjoy a prolonged kiss, knowing it will lead to frantic and fruitless lust; while another couple might decide that peacefully sleeping together naked is a fine way to feel connected while abstaining.

To complicate things further, some behavior could be profoundly loving, emotionally satisfying, and physically pleasant (but not too pleasant!) on one day, and can take the edge off the impatience of waiting, like taking a drink of water to fill the belly while you're waiting for dinner. But you could repeat that exact behavior the next day, with entirely different intentions, and leave one or both spouses feeling used, disgusted, and more frustrated than ever.

This leaves us firmly at the doorstep of the Theology of the Body. One of the main messages of these teachings is: "We speak with our bodies." It can be extremely helpful to ask ourselves frankly, "What am I trying to say?" Am I trying to say, "I love you and want you"? Or, "I want you, and because you love me, you should give me what I want"? Am I trying to say, "I love you and you love me, and our love for each other is more important than our love of God"?

Chastity in marriage is about specific behaviors, but above all, it's about the relationship. So if you're pressuring your spouse to do something that seems wrong to him or her, then that is not chaste behavior, even if it's something that a dating couple could do and still remain in a state of grace. And if your spouse feels rejected and shamed because you're trying to stay chaste, and your attitude is, "Too bad, piggy; I love God more!" then that's not chaste behavior either. Remember, chaste behavior is a positive, not a negative.

Chaste behavior is about a relationship, and a relationship is about love. Yes, sometimes love requires sacrifices. But sacrifices are *for* something. Pursuing chastity is not about giving things up, although it often starts that way. In the end, it's about gaining something. We think of chastity as something austere and painful, or maybe even as a blank: a narrow bed with crisp white sheets and hospital corners, no muss, no fuss, no passion, no fun.

But chastity is more like a garden ready for the sowing—new earth turned up, rocks and roots taken away, ready for sunlight and heavy rains. Learning to be chaste, in other words, is something that makes you ready. It is something that bears fruit.

I am not qualified to tell you about the specifics of what is and is not chaste behavior. But I'm starting to figure out the overarching principle, and it is this: Chastity has as much to do with love as it does with specific body parts. Ignore one aspect or the other, and your behavior is neither loving nor chaste.

You should both be willing to revisit the question, together, of what is and is not acceptable behavior. You should pray about it. You should go to confession when you need to, and you should assume your spouse's best motives as much as possible. And you should talk, talk, talk about it, until you both understand each other better, and you understand the Church's teaching better.

And you should be able to laugh about this a little bit. Mortal sin is no joke, but human beings are hilarious. You're not going to arrive at any great understanding of sexuality if you insist on behaving as if you're Adam and his helpmeet, stiffly cavorting on a faded tapestry. This is why I gave this chapter a name that makes me giggle: because the struggle for chastity is kind of a silly problem to have, and the way we work through it makes us look anything but dignified.

Realize that you are going to mess up. Realize that you're going to need to go to confession as you figure things out. Realize that the priest has heard it before; and realize that that's why marriage is for life: because it takes a lifetime to figure this stuff out.

CHAPTER 17

―――

But What about the Woman?
Part One:
Does God Just Hate Women, or What?

Literature touting NFP always brings up the "honeymoon effect." It goes like this: as the couple abstains in the middle of the cycle, their desire for each other builds up, and they lavish nonsexual attention on each other. Then, when they are finally able to make love, their waiting pays off a thousandfold, and it's a glorious free-for-all of marital, intercoursal, coitalicious bliss.

Unless, of course, you're a woman. Oh, it works out well for some women. But for many others, the "honeymoon effect" is something of a bitter joke—especially if young children, a busy schedule, fluctuating hormones, and plain old fatigue are a regular part of your life. I got this question from a reader:

> What does the Church say about the unfairness to married women, who, when deciding to abstain during fertile times, have to deal with not being able to feel fulfilled every month, but no matter what the time, the guy is always fulfilled?

> It is frustrating when, for the days that she desires her husband, she has to tell her body no, and on the days that she has a green light she doesn't get as much out of the marital embrace. It feels so unfair. The wife is starting to have bitter feelings toward her husband.

Yep. Women generally feel the most sexual desire when they are ovulating. We are made this way because life wants to make more life, and as long as our bodies are ready to make a baby, our bodies are going to try to make us make a baby. And when that window passes, the desire generally decreases (or even drops off so sharply that the idea of sex becomes repellant). Sexual desire in women is also generally lower when we're nursing, because our bodies figure we're not ready for another baby yet—but this time of low desire is the time when we can actually have sex regularly with a low chance of conception.

You can see that this system makes biological sense, and is a strong if unwelcome reminder that, no matter how fancy and civilized we think we are, we're still part of the tribe. The overall benefits to humankind, biologically speaking, are not necessarily compassionate to the individual. All ants want and need to get across the water, but that means some ants have to be the bridge. That's how it is.

That's the first part of the one-two punch. The second part is that women seem to get the short end of the stick theologically, too. After all, since we can't get pregnant without sperm, it's the male orgasm that's super important, right? It's nice if a woman happens to have an orgasm, but The Rules don't bother saying much about it. As long as the man ejaculates inside his wife's vagina, you're covered, spiritually. You're good.

Unless you're the woman. Unless you end up feeling like a handy and theologically airtight sperm receptacle. Too many months of this, and you'll find yourself muttering, "Clearly, God is a man." You know it isn't true that the Church is misogynistic and repressive. It's just that God is. Sex is. Life is. It seems like we women just don't matter at all. It seems like our entire job is to say no when we want to say yes, and yes when we want to say no—and the whole time, everyone's happily caroling about openness to life and the honeymoon effect and marriage-building and pink flowers and hand-holding on the beach. Meanwhile, we're the ones who have to chart, scrupulously planning out our lives so as to carefully avoid any kind of sexual satisfaction. And let's not even talk about pregnancy!

So, yeah. It sucks.

Is this not, then, proof of the hideous, inexcusable misogyny of God? Because so far, everything I've described about sex is true: biologically and theologically, the female orgasm isn't necessary.

But it's only true in the worst possible way, like it's true that music is a progressive array of aural impressions which are culturally desirable and also have been known to produce aidant effects on the limbic system of the brain. That may describe music, but it's certainly not what music is about. It's not what it's supposed to be like. And if music sounds that way to you, then there's either something wrong with you, or with the person playing the music.

I'll paraphrase something Catholic graphic artist Matthew Lickona once said: that men need sex in order to feel loved, and women need to feel loved in order to want to have sex. He said that you can see this situation as just more evidence of the general Unfairness of Things—as some kind of cosmic joke, some kind of Catch-22 that guarantees that everybody will be dissatisfied and left in the lurch.

Or, you could see this arrangement as God's way of making sure we take care of each other—that we step beyond what is easiest, and look to our spouses first.

Because the truth is, the biological and theological inequity of sex is only an unequal burden on the woman when you, as a couple, are doing it wrong. But with some effort, this inequity can actually be the lever which, inserted in the right place, tips the balance in the woman's favor, in a way which is entirely delightful to her husband.

Really.

The rigors of NFP—the self-denial, the dreadful, unasked-for opportunities to build up your married life in ways other than having sex—these are all chances for a husband to start thinking about sex in a new way: to let his wife know that all their days together are precious, and that no real man takes what he wants and considers the deal done.

These are opportunities for a woman to remember that her husband is more vulnerable than he would like to admit: that being a gift to her husband opens up new worlds of happiness for both of them.

These are opportunities for them both to become excellent lovers. These are opportunities for them to start working as one, whether they're having sex or not.

All right, so you can make it work if you try. But why, oh why, does it need to be so complicated? For the longest time, I simply could not understand how God could design the system to be weighted so unfairly against women. Even if it's possible to make the situation better, why design such a backward state of affairs in the first place? It's nice to have a cure, but why engineer the disease?

Eventually I realized: He didn't. Not at all. Why would He? He designed men and women to be different so that they would complement each other. It was original sin that distorted, perverted, and catastrophically skewed this mutuality.

God did not make death, and he does not delight in the death of the living…but through the devil's envy death entered the world. (Wis 1:13; 2:24)

Death includes unhappiness, bitterness, selfishness, dissatisfaction, and animosity. These things were never part of the original design. Something that was meant to be a delicious and fascinating tension between the sexes has devolved into strife and incompatibility, and gets worse from there, without attention.

Anyone who's tuned an instrument knows that two notes in harmony make music; but if one or both are even the faintest shade off their true pitch, then they make a miserable noise. It says in the *Catechism*:

> The harmony in which [men and women] had found themselves, thanks to original justice, is now destroyed: the control of the soul's spiritual faculties over the body is shattered; the union of man and woman becomes subject to tensions, their relations henceforth marked by lust and domination. (400; see Gn 3:7-16)

But when two notes played together sound "off," we don't fix it by trying to make them both play the same note. Instead, we adjust the tension until they are different, but complementary again. This is what we should be striving for in our sexual lives: not equality or fairness, but a rediscovery of complementarity.

Original sin didn't destroy men and women's capability for making each other happy—but it made the goal of complementarity something we have to work toward, not something that happens automatically because of who we are. It hasn't fundamentally changed the character of men and women; but it has put several complications between them.

So, no, God is not a misogynist (and, despite what our hormones may tell us, we're much more than just "part of the tribe"). The Church doesn't hate women. It's not even true that the Church's teaching on human sexuality sadly acknowledges that, from now on, it's gonna suck to be a woman.

On the contrary: the Church's teaching on human sexuality is the *cure* to the damage done by original sin. As it says in one of the Preface prayers at Mass:

For we know it belongs to your boundless glory,
that you came to the aid of mortal beings with your
        divinity
and even fashioned for us a remedy out of
        mortality itself,
that the cause of our downfall
might become the means of our salvation.

This is how God works. He does not want us to suffer. He never designed us to be in conflict with each other. But since that's how the world is now, He comes to our rescue, offering the very cause of our suffering "as the means of our salvation."

If men and women are divided, it is through this division that He will bring us back together, to restore us to the complementarity and harmony for which we were designed.

CHAPTER 18

But What about the Woman?
Part Two:
So What Do We Do about It?

In the last section, I talked a little bit about how it's God's plan that men get to have all the fun, and women just have to put up with it, because then they get holy.

Ha ha, just kidding! If you think that's what I said, go back and read it again—especially the parts about opportunities and hard work. If a woman feels bitter and unhappy and used, even if the couple is doing everything right theologically, then this is not what God wants. It is not what the Church wants. And, most importantly, it should not be what the husband wants.

Here are two important points:

First, if you improve your relationship outside the bedroom, your sex life will almost always get better. Women tend to be more aware of this link, but it's just as true for men: a better sex life comes from being more unified as a couple in general. So, the woman who wrote the question in the last chapter, who said she is beginning to feel bitter and resentful? I would bet you a trillion dollars that she also feels resentful about other things in their relationship, and isn't merely keeping score of his vs. her orgasms.

If a woman feels used, put-upon, taken for granted, under-valued, or just plain overworked in her daily life, then these emotions tamp out sexual desire effectively and cumulatively.

If, on the other hand, she feels appreciated, cherished, admired, and sought-after (in the best way), and generally like someone whose happiness matters, then it is amazing how much easier it is to overcome hormonally-based disinclinations and fatigue. "Yes, my dear. I'm tired. *But not that tired!*"

Is it a man's responsibility to make it impossible for his wife to be unhappy? Of course not. Sometimes it's his behavior that needs to change; but sometimes it's hers. Most of the time, it's both of theirs: if she's unhappy, he needs to put more effort into making her happier, and she needs to put more effort into being reasonable and contented.

So that's the first point: the quality of your sex life is often about everything else in your life besides sex.

The second extremely important point that you need to keep in mind if you want to improve your sex life is: nothing will get better if you don't talk about it. How could it? Men don't know what it's like to be women, and women don't know what it's like to be men. The only way they will find out is to tell each other, and to listen attentively to one other.

But couples often need to learn how to talk about things. Many women feel that they're expert talkers, and if their husbands would just sit and listen, they would explain everything they need to know and life would be fine; and many men feel that when things are bad, the one thing that will make it worse is to talk about it. The truth is, women usually have less to say than they think they do, and men have more to say than they want to admit. The key is learning how to make space around these conversations so that they are productive. (For more about this skill, see "How to Have a Difficult Conversation with Your Husband.") But if there is a problem, it simply will not be solved, ever, unless you understand each other's point of view.

Take, for instance, the situation I described above, where a woman can't have sex when she wants to, and doesn't want to when she can—whereas a man can have it, and like it, any time. Sounds like it's exclusively a woman's problem, right?

But think about this: it's only marginally easier for a man to live that way. Look at his month: on the days when his wife is attracted to him, when she is most attractive to him, and when she will be the most responsive and unencumbered and joyful in bed—these are the days when he is supposed to say, lovingly, "No sweat, I can wait!" But on the days when she's less confident, more moody, less in tune with her own body and his, and possibly going through the motions out of a sense of duty, or making herself unavailable altogether—these are the times when he can go to town.

Yay.

So much for "guaranteed fulfillment." Yes, he gets an orgasm. No, this doesn't mean he's getting everything he wants or needs. It would be sort of like getting all the hot fudge sundaes you want, but never getting a good square meal. It may be fun at first, but after a while, it's just as unsatisfying as going hungry.

If he is a narcissist, or immature, or simply clueless or lacking experience, then this situation may not bother him at all.

But most men grow out of that as the couple gradually learns how a sexual relationship works. Most men don't want to be thrown a scrap out of pity or a sense of duty. They want to be pleased, and they want to give pleasure. They want to learn how to become amazing lovers—by actually learning techniques, learning timing, learning about the element of surprise, learning about the power of words and breath, learning what to do with their hands and their mouths and their whole bodies, and not just their pelvises. Learning their wives' bodies. Learning their wives' hearts.

And men want to be wanted. It's not just that they like getting off, and that they also, as a separate notion, like seeing their wives happy: no, it's all part of the same thing. Adult men are clear on the fact that bringing a woman to orgasm is an indispensible part of being masculine. Any dum-dum can ejaculate, but giving a women genuine pleasure and satisfaction is what separates the boys from the men.

So the problem is that, when you're fertile but need to avoid pregnancy, the levels of desire and the days of opportunity match up exactly wrong.

There are two ways to solve this problem. The first (which only works if you enjoy sex during pregnancy) is just to go ahead and conceive, if you can. If a chart-induced clash of libidos is just killing you, it might make you reevaluate your reasons for postponing pregnancy. So think hard! Do you really need to put a baby off right now? You aren't going to be fertile forever, and it's hard to imagine saying, five years later, "Boy, I really regret having that one particular kid."

But of course, sometimes there is a good reason to work through the challenges. Pregnancy is a beautiful thing, but sometimes it's just not the right time to have a baby; and sometimes pregnancy can have the effect of masking marital problems, or kicking them down the road. Sometimes, you need to hunker down and face your problems head on.

So the second solution is to work toward a place where the woman's problem is her husband's problem. Even just knowing that he takes her suffering seriously and personally is a tremendous step toward closing the rift between them.

So this problem—the disastrous mismatch of desire and timing—is a perfect example of the kind of hardship that can lead to greater understanding than you might achieve if there were no problem in the first place...if you work on understanding each other, rather than just stewing in your differentness. If the husband or the wife is unhappy about some aspect of their sexual life, then the only way to solve it is to address it as a joint problem—because, in marriage, all problems are joint problems, just as all joys are shared joys.

It's helpful to realize that women are often just as guilty as men of imbibing the cultural lie that sex is all about bodies. It's not. Most men have an emotional life which is just as highly developed as a woman's—and most men will not feel satisfied unless there is some kind of emotional satisfaction during sex. But they may be less willing to admit, even to themselves, that this is the case. And so there can be a vicious cycle: the woman isn't satisfied, and feels used, which makes her less responsive, which makes him feel unwanted, which makes him less willing to go the extra mile to satisfy her, which makes her feel used, which makes her less responsive...

Here is what the Church asks of us, beyond the mechanics of what our bodies may and may not do: a man should work with his wife to figure out what he can do for her so that she feels close enough to want to have sex, even when she isn't biologically primed to seek it out.

And the Church asks a woman to work with her husband to figure out what she can do for him so that he feels cared-for and desired even when the stars are not in their favor, whether they're having sex or not.

The Church asks men and women to put aside their own easy desires and to think of their spouses first. It asks them, in short, to become expert lovers.

So what kinds of things can we actually do to improve our love lives, emotionally and physically? Well, you don't have to re-invent the wheel. You just have to figure out how you work together as a specific, unique couple. Here are the things you should try to find out about each other (probably not all in a single conversation, though!):

- What kind of foreplay is pleasant? What feels good, what feels weird, what do you wish for?
- What about specific positions? What about what we say to each other, what we wear? How do you feel about lin-

gerie and sex toys?[1] How can we learn more about these things without heading into dangerous waters?

- How do you feel after sex? Satisfied? Unhappy? Guilty or confused? What can I do to make it better?
- How have we noticed these things changing at various times of the cycle? Do we fall into ruts or predictably bad behavior at certain times? Can we anticipate these problems and try something different, to head them off next time?
- What is the major disagreement we have outside the bedroom? Is it manifesting itself in our sex lives? Is this something we have control over? If not, can we make some compromises?
- Do we have reasonable expectations about our sex life, according to our particular current schedule, age, and physical health?
- Have we thoroughly researched the treatable causes of sexual problems? Is solo or couples counseling called for? What about hormone or dietary supplements?
- What can I do during the day to make the nighttime something to look forward to? What can I do during the time of abstinence to make our sex life better?
- What is abstinence like for you? What can I do to make it better next time?
- What is pregnancy like? What is living with a pregnant woman like? How do we feel about another baby right now? How can we handle the next pregnancy and postpartum stage better than we did last time?

---

[1] There is a wide range of products that could be called "sex toys." Some are objectively immoral; but some are morally neutral, and, depending on how they are used, they could be true "marital aids," or true disasters. This is why, if your sex life involves anything besides your two nakes bodies, I recommend discussing it thoroughly, being honest about what effect these things have on you as a couple, and praying about any uncertainty you have.

- Overall, do you feel like I understand you?
- When was the last time we prayed together, about sex, babies, or about anything?
- Do you know how much I love you? What can I do to show it to you?

In other words, you need to talk about all of those things that you thought you could do without, back when you were a horny young thing and you were *so in love*.

These conversations will probably continue throughout your marriage.

The good news is, these conversations get easier as you get to know each other better. Not only will you work your way through problems, but you will get better at talking about them. Someday you'll be elated to realize that you just quickly dealt with a problem which, years ago, would have been fodder for a month-long fight. Talking it out will be hard at first; but as you discover more and more about your beloved, it may actually become a pleasure.

Having these conversations means having the courage and the sense of self-worth to ask extraordinary things of each other. It means having the courage and humility to assess whether you're doing anything extraordinary for your spouse.

So, to sum up: in order to reap the relationship benefits of NFP, we must work on the entire relationship, and we must learn to communicate and behave in a more loving way. Is that all?

No, not really.

The Church asks one more thing: that we embrace the Cross. It's good to serve your spouse when you know that there will be some sort of payoff that you can both enjoy. But at some point, you're going to have to serve God, period, even when there seems to be no hope of any reward in this life—even if this spouse, whose joys and burdens you share, is causing you pain.

You're not going to get away from the Cross. This is true whether you're male or female or single or married or deployed or divorced or gay or impotent or several of the above. There is no way of arranging your life so that you will be free of suffering. Sometimes, things don't turn out the way we like. Being an adult in the faith means desiring the good of other people more than your own satisfaction—even if they themselves don't want that good for themselves.

It can be helpful to realize that it's a conscious choice to embrace the Cross. After all, a woman can easily go on birth control, with or without her husband's knowledge. A man can get a vasectomy without his wife's approval. Anyone can turn to porn or online flirtations for relief. Couples can masturbate, mutually or alone, so that you at least get some fun out of those days of peak fertility. But you have chosen not to (or you keep repenting, if you do give in to these temptations). In today's culture, that practically makes you a hero! I'm not even kidding. So give yourself some credit: you're doing something truly difficult, and you're doing it because you choose to. Recognize that it's a choice, and own it.

Here's the thing: God doesn't give us crosses because He wants us to be unhappy. He doesn't say, "Carry your cross and shut your mouth." He says, "Shoulder my yoke and learn from Me."

Suffering, but also learning. What we learn from the Cross of NFP is how to give ourselves to each other, and how to give ourselves, as a couple, to God. At a wedding, this looks lovely: the groom and bride in black and white, a pair of golden rings, each speaking in turn, both being toasted by a happy crowd.

In everyday life, giving yourself to each other sometimes means giving over your body, or giving over your desires in favor of your spouse's desires. It also means giving up your ideas of what your spouse wants. It might mean giving up your idea of what sex is for, or what love means. It might mean giving up your idea of what you're actually working toward, when you work on improving your sex life.

Most of the time, giving these things up is no loss. Most of the time, they are replaced by something more solid—and often, by something more joyful.

But sometimes, a sacrifice just plain hurts. That's what makes it a sacrifice. But even then, it is not for nothing. How could it be, when any pain can be united with Christ's?

So, to return to our original question: No, the Church does not hate women. Her teaching shows that she fully understands a woman's desires—and that she fully expects a man to work until he does the same (and vice versa). She sets things up so that a man and a woman both have something to strive for. And ultimately, she gives us a supreme opportunity for realigning our souls so that we look forward, toward heaven.

Mother Church never sends us away empty when we follow her commandments. But, like any good mother, she doesn't give her children everything they want—and this is true for men and for women. We all want to be satisfied. But sometimes what we crave is not the same as what we need.

CHAPTER 19

How to Have a Difficult
Conversation with Your Husband

It's unavoidable: you're going to have to talk about sex. Even worse, you're going to have to find a way to get your husband to talk about sex. Even the most communicative couples could use some tips for making the most of what can be an awkward or painful conversation (and those tips apply to any difficult conversation, not just ones about sex).

Now, I don't mean to give the impression that if women just follow some simple guidelines, healing will magically occur in a deeply troubled marriage. Sometimes, couples understand each other perfectly well, and they simply don't agree—and, when their disagreement is serious enough, prayer is their only recourse. Not all problems can be fixed.

On the other hand, it's common for good relationships to go through times when pain outweighs the joy. But it's also common to come out of the bad patches stronger and more united than you were when things were chugging along peacefully. So here are a few ideas for how to approach your untalkative husband when there's something wrong:

Don't ambush him. If you're upset about something, you're likely to let it burst out in a moment that is already highly emotionally charged, and it won't go well. You will get much better results if you give him warning that you need to discuss something difficult, and even set an appointment (or, better, ask him when he will be free to talk about it).

Decide ahead of time specifically what you want to talk about, and stick to that. Even if you have other, perfectly legitimate complaints, it's not helpful (or accurate) to give the impression that you think he's a failure in every possible way. Put your complaint in this context: "You are so great about X, Y, and Z, and it helps me so much in ways R, S, and T. But can we talk about Q?"

Make it safe for him to respond. Even if your husband fully understands that there's a problem and wants to resolve it, it will be almost impossible for him to open his mouth if everything he says is met with screams of grief, immediate counterarguments, or ridicule. If you say you want to know what's on his mind, but then get hysterical when you hear it, he will have no choice but to try to protect both of you by shutting up. Try with all your might to listen quietly, and make only encouraging responses.

(I do not mean to imply that he should always be shielded from your pain if he's done something wrong. It's important that he understands how much he's hurt you. But if your immediate goal is to encourage him to talk, then try to be restrained during that conversation. He won't talk if he's drowning in your tears.)

Don't ask questions that you don't need to know the answer to. Even if you're burning with curiosity to know how his mind works, consider how it will affect your state of mind if you know the worst. Sometimes you will decide you gotta know; but sometimes you may admit that you can live without finding out certain things. Whether the question is, "Did you sleep with my sister?" or "Do you like this nightgown?" be honest with yourself about how strong you are right now—maybe this question can wait.

His eyes are up here. Don't look into them. A face-to-face posture may foster honesty between women, but some men find it antagonistic. Know your husband's preference. It may be easier to go for a walk or sit side-by-side; and it may help to hold hands, for that tactile reminder that you're on the same side, even when you're angry.

Be prepared to be wrong. Even if you're the most victimized, wounded, injured party in the world, you're not completely innocent—no one is. Own up to your contribution to the problem, no matter how slight. You're in this together.

Remember that he hasn't been living inside your head. You may be talking about a grievance that you've been stewing over for months, but to him, it might be new material. Maybe you've been rehearsing the conversation mentally, and already know how he ought to respond—but he's not privy to your script. Give your words time to sink in. Sometimes men seem to brush off an idea the first time they hear it, only to come back two weeks later and say, "Okay, here is what I think."

Don't expect to get to the bottom of things in one session. Even if it's a groundbreaking conversation, think of it as one in a series, and be patient. If it's hard for your husband to talk, then it will be even harder for him to keep on talking; so be content that you've made a start, and be alert for the next suitable time to bring up the topic. If today's conversation is over, it's over.

Consider his family of origin. Was he mocked, chastised, or swatted down for expressing himself? That kind of training stays with a person. Make it clear to your husband that your house is not his childhood house, and be patient.

Pray for a fruitful conversation before you begin. I once overheard a priest praying quietly, "Help me say what You want me to say, and help them hear what You want them to hear." He was preparing to give a sermon, but this seems like a useful prayer for a conversation between spouses, too. The grace of the sacrament of marriage is real, but you have to keep asking God to top it off throughout your life together.

CHAPTER 20

How to Help Your Husband with NFP

Women are usually happy to talk about NFP. They are pretty clear about what they wish their husbands would do to make things easier, and they're not shy about sharing that information. You often hear women saying, "I know my husband is frustrated, and I feel bad, but I don't know what to do." Men often want to protect their wives, even to the point of damaging their relationship: they think that if they say nothing, then there is no problem, even when there clearly is a problem.

So one day, I asked a bunch of Catholic men to anonymously share some ideas about how their wives could help them when they're struggling with NFP. Their words were overwhelming. It was hard not to feel defensive, and some of the men had truly unreasonable expectations: they wanted their wives to supply everything, and thought only in terms of women's duty and men's gratification.

But those guys were in the minority. Most of these good Catholic men had small requests, and clearly wanted their wives to be happy. Most of them wanted to improve their marriages, and hoped it was possible. Most of them thought their wives (even the old, tired, out-of-shape ones!) were genuinely beautiful and genuinely desirable, and these men weren't sure how to communicate that idea. And most of them had a deep longing to be understood.

Here are some of their suggestions about how their wives can help them with NFP.

How to Help—On Days of Abstinence

Don't mock the poor guy. If your husband is suffering, don't mock or shrug off his difficulty. Imagine being told that, for a big chunk of the month, you weren't allowed to talk to him, hug him, or hear him speak your name. Think of something you'd miss horribly—something that would make you feel isolated and unattached. Now imagine being teased or belittled for feeling that way. Don't do that to your husband, even if you can't see why it's so hard for him to abstain.

One man explained: "It is the perceived indifference to our plight, and even mockery of it, that cuts men to the quick."

Another husband observed: "One of the huge problems for a guy is that, if his wife can't understand and respect his struggle in this particular sacrifice, then who can? Society and the media are bombarding us with ridicule of men and the ways they commonly receive love, while telling us all to value and respect women's needs. In answer to this dilemma, guys are simply told to 'deal with it' in private, or, in Catholic circles, to 'offer it up.'"

And another: "The times I've done the best are when my wife has shared with me how proud she is that I am trying, how much it means to her that I love her enough to do this, and that she gets how tough it is. Times when she is empathetic to my struggle. Those efforts on her part are an incredible source of strength."

Learn how to be intimate with your clothes on. Non-sexual intimacy is a skill that must be learned, especially if you were sexually active before you were married. Cultivating other kinds of intimacy can make abstaining less painful, as well as enhancing sex.

It's not what you do, it's how you do it. It doesn't need to be elaborate. You don't even have to leave the house, as long as you spend some time focused only on each other, without the kids, once or twice a week. Plan a date: dinner, a movie, or a TV night. Or turn off the TV (and all other screens), and work together, go for a walk together, play cards, or have a beer. Plan ahead to make sure it happens. Hiding from one another, even with good intentions, is poison for a marriage.

One husband said:

> I have to say that the only success I've had is when, instead of pulling away, I enter the breach and work on the relationship and intimacy just when the tension is highest. Does this make times of abstinence easy? Well, yes and no. It was still challenging, but all the bitterness and angst I usually associate with abstinence was mostly missing. And the closeness I was feeling to my wife, well, that was a really wonderful thing. The tension of abstaining was still there fairly regularly, but the intimacy from other sources made the pill sweet rather than bitter to swallow.

Talk about your own desire, and ask for his help. When you are abstaining, let him know that you wish you could be having sex (and some husbands say it's okay to exaggerate a bit); and appeal to his protective side.

One husband explained: "Emotionally, it's reassuring to know that she's interested. Also, it can serve to deflect a man's thoughts from himself to how he can help his wife. To be honest, abstaining is no pleasure, but how much more difficult must it be that the period of abstaining, for a woman, comes when her body is most geared up. Turning a man's thoughts from self-pity to self-donation can only be for the good."

Don't tempt him. Don't start something you're not willing to finish. Find out what gets him going, and don't do that—whether it's dress, or behavior, or words—if you're supposed to be abstaining. It may help to make a list together of dos and don'ts, which may need to be adjusted over time. But be prudent here! Sometimes naming All Those Kinds of Things out loud can be a temptation in itself. (Here's a good opportunity to laugh at yourselves, which never hurts.)

How to Help—When Abstinence Is Over

Just do it. I know, you're tired. But give the guy a break—he's your husband, not some jerk at a bar. Even if it wasn't in your plans, have sex as often as you can on the available part of the month. He shouldn't have to beg.

It may seem like it's exhaustion or hormonal problems that are squelching your drive, but a lack of physical desire can also come from emotional distress masquerading as other difficulties. If you work to improve the relationship, your desire may increase.

Prepare. Don't pick infertile days for your most enormous, tiring projects. On days where you can have sex, let your schedule be geared toward the evening and your husband. As much as possible, plan accordingly, and don't stay up too late the night before.

Some men appreciate a clean bedroom, and many women get in the mood when they feel beautiful. Take some time to fix your hair, paint your nails, or go ahead and buy some sexy underwear. Most women are much more critical of their own bodies than their husbands are, so don't be shy about dressing up.

How to Help—Anytime

Spruce up. None of the men I talked to said, "I wish my wife were younger and thinner." But they did say they like it when their wives dress up a little for them. If you put on earrings or a clean shirt to go out shopping, then you can do it for your husband, too.

Do nice things for him. Maybe you feel like you already do nice things. You cook for his tastes, you wash his clothes, you bear his children…what more could he want?

Well, he wants to know that you like him.

Find out what makes your husband happy, and do something extra for him each day. Cook something special, give him a sweet note or an unexpected compliment, or jump up to get him seconds on coffee. When he gets home, stop what you're doing and make a fuss over him. It's not June Cleaver; it's love.

Communicate clearly. Let him know as early as you can what the daily fertility status is. If you have determined that the use of NFP is God's will for your marriage right now, take it seriously! Chart flawlessly, or at least make sure you're on the same page about how serious you need to be. If your beloved is going to be annoyed, let it be at the system, not at you.

Pray together. Pray together every day, and state your intentions out loud. This can be one of the most breathtakingly intimate activities of your married life. If you regularly pray together for a more chaste and joyful intimate life, then God will probably give it to you.

And privately pray for your husband's happiness daily. You may find yourself becoming the answer to that prayer.

But enough about him…what about you?

You're the one who has to chart, menstruate, gestate, and lactate, not to mention clean the bathroom. Never mind helping your husband—what about the ways he can make NFP easier for you?

Well, there are two reasons that list isn't in this chapter.

The first reason is that I'm pretty sure you already have your own list. If there is something you want your husband to know, for heaven's sake tell him; he can't read your mind. Often, it's misunderstandings that cause trouble, not malice. It's okay to insist on having some conversations about how your husband can help you, as long as you're ready to hear his side, too.

The second reason to focus more on what you can do to help him is because of the "unitive" part of your love life. That's not over-spiritualized happy talk: it's what intimacy is about, and it's just as important as making babies.

Your husband's problems are your problems, and his happiness will likely lead to your happiness, sometimes in unexpected ways. Bad sex comes from bad relationships, and generally not vice versa.

Even if you aren't getting along, and you wish he would treat you better, force yourself to take the first step—treat him a little better, and see where it leads.

If he doesn't want to talk about it, try presenting it this way: "I want to have a better, more active sex life with you." You can even go over this essay together, and ask him which ideas ring true, and which don't. Maybe none will, but at least you will be talking about it. Each man is unique, but every couple is the same in one way: they really must talk about these things.

The truth is, all the hype about natural family planning is true. The benefits are real; it's just that they're not inevitable. It takes practice, and it takes effort to gain them. You will probably get an awful lot wrong before you get anything right. But if you do make the effort, you will be rewarded with a stronger marriage, a more satisfying intimate life, and a whole lot of help toward greater holiness along the way.

CHAPTER 21

What's So Natural about
Natural Family Planning?

"Natural" family planning, eh? Couples who are disenchanted with NFP often laugh morosely over the name. How can you call it "natural" when you can't just love freely, but have to consult a chart? How can you call it "natural" when, on the days when a woman is feeling frisky and ready to go, those are the days they have to abstain? So it's not enough that she's at the beck and call of an infant—she has to wake up and attend to a fertility monitor first thing in the morning? It's not enough that a man has to provide for his wife's emotional and physical well-being—now he has to plan around the position of her cervix, too?

How can you call it "natural" when a married couple has to make a clinical note of every time they have sex? And if someone travels for work, or gets deployed, it's almost guaranteed that the infertile days will very perfectly, precisely, and predictably fail to line up with the days you're actually together. And let's not even talk about how well natural family planning cooperates with Valentine's Day or anniversaries. Let's raise a glass to our married bliss—and then put the glass back down.

Suddenly our marital boudoir becomes an accountant's portfolio of charts and numbers, gadgets, stress, and uncertainty. "Doin' what comes naturally" is exactly what we're not supposed to do, if we're trying to avoid pregnancy.

Natural, my ass.

But listen, it's not going to make anything easier if you re-name it "Stupid, Aggravating Family Planning Designed to Make Me Suffer," even if that's how you feel. The problem here is that we associate the word "natural" with a sort of fuzzy concept of ease and simplicity and wholesome goodness: something intuitive and earthy, possibly involving handcrafted sandals and bread with a lot of seeds and nutty bits in it.

Now, natural family planning does have something to do with this kind of "natural." Because it doesn't use hormones (or plastic, or metal, or latex, or sponges, or gels, or implants, or coils, or inserts, or scalpels) that end up polluting the public water supply and poisoning the body, it's green, organic, and entirely natural. And that in itself is a good and worthy thing.

But here's the main point: when we say "natural family planning," we mean it has to do with the nature of things—the true nature, for instance, of sex. It's the only method of managing fertility that does not interfere in any way in the function of fertility. It simply attempts to define it by saying, "Look here, lady, these are the days when your body is up to something. Make of it what you will."

When a couple keeps a chart, and they realize the woman may be fertile, and they decide to have sex anyway, and then the wom-an gets pregnant, they often get mad at the system. This makes about as much sense as seeing a sign that says "thin ice," deciding to risk it, falling in the water, and getting mad at the sign.

Most often, people who are mad at NFP are actually mad at sex. Most modern people are fairly used to being bailed out, one way or another. Many types of escape have become routine: debt forgiveness, exam retakes, and appeals processes of every kind. There's always someone to call if you've made a bad choice. There's always some way out, or at least someone else to blame.

If you are pro-life, though, and you have sex on a fertile day when you didn't want to get pregnant, there is no appeals process.

The chart says what it says, and the rest is up to you. And that sucks.

So NFP baldly reveals the nature of the procreative aspect of sex: it doesn't matter what your extenuating circumstances are. This is biology and morality wedded together in one unyielding truth: sex is for making babies.

It doesn't matter what emotional baggage you have, or what your psychological reasons for accidentally thinking it was day four when it was really only day three: you did it, and now you're pregnant. We can all see how *that's* fair, even if we don't like it.

But what about method failure, when you follow the rules to avoid pregnancy, and get pregnant anyway? It does happen. Or what about charts that are so tricky it takes consultation with experts to figure out when conception occurred—when it's only in retrospect that you can say, "Oh, well you shouldn't have used this day"? Is it in any way fair to say that the couple is at fault for ignoring the facts, when they were doing their absolute best to play by the rules, and the rules failed them?

Nope. It's not fair.

But this is also part of the true nature of sex: it's not about being fair. It's about something more than justice. It's about love.

Many couples can skate through their sex life without ever having to face the beyond-fairness of sex. NFP seems fair to them: follow the rules, and get what you planned. They find charting simple and effective, and perhaps look askance at couples who grouse and complain or end up getting pregnant at the stupidest times.

But many couples discover something that no other aspect of their life managed to hammer home: that fair treatment is something of a cage. Remember the older Eucharistic prayer, where we begged God, "Do not consider what we truly deserve." This is what we encounter, when we encounter Love: God, who is Love, wants to give us something more than fairness—something better.

But no, not always something easier.

When I say "love," I don't mean how you feel. I don't mean affection or desire or closeness or bliss or contentment. I mean love in a fallen world, which sometimes looks like a fiery sword banning you from the garden. Or love that sometimes looks like a Cross. There you hang, trying with all your might to remember why you're doing this, and not knowing how much longer it's going to go on. Sometimes when love speaks, it asks, "Why have you abandoned me?"

These are the things that I have learned while learning NFP, and I thank God that I've learned them: NFP is natural because it reveals the nature of our marriage. It makes us face up to just how selfish we can be. Enough to push our wives into getting pregnant just so we can feel satisfied? Enough to make our husbands feel like superfluous frat boys just because they want to feel loved?

It reveals the nature of our plans—how negotiable they really are. Do we need to postpone a pregnancy, truly, if it's going to be this difficult? Maybe not. Sometimes difficulty clarifies things.

And sometimes realizing that the road you've chosen is a demanding one gives you the courage to stay on that road.

It reveals the nature of our relationship with God. It sounds cute and comforting to say "God is in control," and people who say that may imagine sitting on Daddy's lap behind the wheel of the family car, going "Vroom vroomy vroom!" while Daddy does the steering. In reality, when God is in control, it feels more like one of those movies where some amateur has to step up and land the airplane or steer the ship to safety through a crashing storm, with an expert giving them instructions remotely through a headset. In theory, following the expert's instructions will help us get in safely; but our fear, panic, self-doubt, and lack of skill are not exactly comforting. Yes, God is in control, but we're the ones who are in for a rough ride.

It reveals the nature of our relationship with the world—with skeptical doctors, worried or disgusted family members, and sneering progressives who imagine that we're just too dumb to figure out how to unwrap a condom. Just how much can we stand to be misunderstood, as long as we know we're doing the right thing? Just how are we going to balance material demands and priorities with eternal ones? Just how weird are we willing to appear?

You can find out these things about sex, about yourself, about God, and about the world without ever opening a chart, of course. And you can spend an entire marriage charting without learning a damn thing.

But the information is there. Do with it what you will.

Spacing pregnancies typically requires people to abstain when they don't want to abstain, and it often requires people to step up and show love even if they're not swept up in spontaneous passion. It requires people to be dedicated to a higher goal than their own happiness: namely, the well-being of their spouse and the strength of their family life. This is what's known as "love."

We are made to love. It's in our nature. And that is why it's called "natural family planning."

ACKNOWLEDGMENTS

———————

Eighty-one percent of Americans feel they have a book in them. Most of these folks can be cured of that feeling by increasing fluids and upping their fiber intake. I wasn't so lucky, and needed lots of help getting the damn thing out.

My sincere thanks to Susie Bright, the best editor I've ever met, for her endless patience, encouragement, honesty, and a little bit of cussing;

To my old friends on the Delphi NFP board, who gave me so many stories, and such a brilliant example of Catholic sisterhood;

To Jennifer Fulwiler and Danielle Bean, two of the busiest women in the world, who somehow always had time to cheer me on;

To my sister, Abby Tardiff, who read this book, edited it, steered me away from a few disasters, and wrestled Microsoft Word into submission;

To John Herreid, who donated his time and expertise to design this book's hilarious cover;

To my kids, who held the baby for a minute so I could go write a book;

And to my husband, Damien, the only man alive who can make me stop talking and just be happy.